THE PAST AS LIBERATION FROM HISTORY

COUNTERPOINTS

STUDIES IN THE POSTMODERN THEORY OF EDUCATION

JOE L. KINCHELOE AND SHIRLEY R. STEINBERG
GENERAL EDITORS

VOL. 63

PETER LANG
New York • Washington, D.C./Baltimore • Boston • Bern
Frankfurt am Main • Berlin • Brussels • Vienna • Canterbury

SCOTT P. CULCLASURE

THE PAST AS LIBERATION FROM HISTORY

PETER LANG
New York • Washington, D.C./Baltimore • Boston • Bern
Frankfurt am Main • Berlin • Brussels • Vienna • Canterbury

Library of Congress Cataloging-in-Publication Data

Culclasure, Scott P.
The past as liberation from history / Scott P. Culclasure.
p. cm. — (Counterpoints; vol. 63)
Includes bibliographical references.
1. History—Philosophy. 2. History—Study and teaching (Higher)—
United States. I. Title. II. Series: Counterpoints (New York, N.Y.); vol. 63.
D16.8.C78 901—dc21 98-30526
ISBN 0-8204-3840-5
ISSN 1058-1634

Die Deutsche Bibliothek-CIP-Einheitsaufnahme

Culclasure, Scott P.:
The past as liberation from history / Scott P. Culclasure.
–New York; Washington, D.C./Baltimore; Boston; Bern;
Frankfurt am Main; Berlin; Brussels; Vienna; Canterbury: Lang.
(Counterpoints; Vol. 63)
ISBN 0-8204-3840-5

Cover design by Nona Reuter

"Straws, and sticks, and dust with most are the great things now looked after."

John Bunyan, *The Pilgrim's Progress, Second Part* (1684)

Contents

Preface

When what had been my dissertation was accepted for publication, I was naturally delighted. But when Shirley Steinberg of Peter Lang Publishing suggested how to revise this early work, my delight was compounded, for without knowing my background she asked me to write what I had wanted but had not been able to accommodate within my doctoral work: how I taught history in a public high school. The resulting book, therefore, reflects an approach that in its first part might be described as somewhat theoretical and abstract, and in its second as more practical and concrete. If I have learned anything after many years of teaching, it is that these two approaches, instead of existing in opposition to each other, are necessary compliments. Teachers routinely complain, with too much justification, of education courses taught by professors who are far removed from "real" classroom experiences and too enthralled by the world of ideas; I suspect professors are equally suspicious of teachers who appear unwilling to question why they do what they do on the grounds that the reasons are perfectly obvious and too simple to pursue.

The earliest part of this work was nurtured by a dissertation committee that belied the stereotype of cranky, impossible-to-please professors. I am enormously grateful to them for allowing me free reign. They are Svi Shapiro, who chaired the committee and always welcomed me back when I returned from the wilderness with another chapter; Robert M. Calhoon, a quietly insightful historian who remained unflappable in the midst of "educators"; Ceola Ross Baber, who constantly challenged me to see things from different perspectives; and David Purpel, who asked for paragraphs when I was too easily satisfied with sentences.

At Peter Lang Publishing I enjoyed the enthusiasm of Christopher S. Myers and series editors Joe Kincheloe and Shirley Steinberg. First Nona Reuter and then Jacqueline Pavlovic guided the production of this book and patiently answered my questions every step of the way.

Once again, I owe more than I can convey to my wife Nancy Newton Culclasure; suffice it to say that I better understand why the Book of Proverbs speaks of Wisdom in a feminine voice. I think this effort has been worthwhile; I hope she, and one day,

Alice and David, will agree.

Last, I remember the many wonderful students I have been privileged to teach and acknowledge that without them, I would never have been inspired to do better.

Introduction

Past as Present

Perhaps southerners, living in a land that has experienced both great destructiveness in the past and a headlong rush into the present, possess a heightened sense of loss and dislocation. Certainly the novelist Ellen Glasgow keenly felt how the past can unexpectedly pervade the present, describing as she did Asa Timberlake's state as he watched the house of his childhood being torn down:

> They will never again build like this, he thought. Dignity is an anachronism. Yes, the old house was going out with its age, with its world, with its manners, with its fashion in architecture.
>
> Suddenly, it seemed to him that stillness was gathering without and within. He stood alone in a lost hemisphere, while time flowed on above, around, and beyond him. Muffled discords from the present, now near, now far, rushed toward him, assailed his ears, and dropped back in the tumult. He heard cars speeding, horns blowing, feet hurrying, voices calling, dogs barking, radios crooning, starlings chattering as they settled to roost. Then, while he listened, the sounds dwindled; the moment broke up and vanished. . . .[1]

Glasgow believed her theme to be universal: that "the modern temper, as it pressed round me, in a single community, appeared confused, vacillating, uncertain, and distracted from permanent values," traits that characterized a community caught "between an age that is slipping out and an age that is hastening in."[2]

Glasgow's last novels were written at a time when the contrast between two ages was especially poignant. The 1,845 Civil War veterans who gathered for the seventy-fifth Gettysburg reunion in 1938 were treated with the spectacle of a simulated air attack by B-17 bombers. Like the protagonists in Glasgow's novels, we also live in seemingly dissolving communities where we grasp "frantically at the running shadow of happiness."[3] Unsettled by a life in which all the old certainties—family, faith, work, an identity secure in these things—seem to be dissolving, we suspect that others are robbing us, yet who, and in what manner, we cannot exactly say.

The public schools are especially well-situated to witness and, sadly, contribute to the alienation of individuals from each other and their community by helping to carry the banner proclaiming that our greatest responsibility is to foster economic competitiveness, heedless of capitalism's dislocating effects. While those of us who work in schools cannot be held responsible for every affliction public education suffers, we should be expected to recognize that by failing to ask why schools are as they are, we may be passing judgments on our students that we would deprecate if they were more forthrightly articulated.

I have been a history teacher for long enough that, whatever other work I may do, I will probably always think of myself as one. Much of the thoughtful time in my career has been devoted to learning history, but, as I matured, much has also been given to learning *about* history. The social construction we call history is essential in satisfying our ingrained desire for the past to explain who we are. The histories we tell, however, too often deny stories that contradict the progressive, optimistic view of our culture we like to portray in a public school setting. Ironically, it is these very stories, tragic as they are, that we most need to recall, not for the pointless exercise of making us feel ashamed, but to cause us to question whether society's present arrangement of power is the most equitable we can hope for. We turn to the richness and variety of the past to find the empowering identities that our more narrowly conceived histories frequently deny us—hence the title of this book.

This book is divided into two parts in order to distinguish the first four chapters, which tend toward philosophical concerns, from the more concrete examples elaborated in the last four chapters. If the first part speaks to my orientation toward education, the second part addresses my practice as a teacher. The effect I desire is contrapuntal, in which theory and practice harmonize with each other while retaining their own individual lines of thought.

In Part I, "Underpinnings," Chapter 1, "A Personal Account of Fashioning History," demonstrates how selective and incomplete even the best-intentioned histories are by describing the inevitable gaps appearing in my attempt to arrange the fragmented knowledge of my family's history. Not only must we struggle with the incompleteness of our knowledge, we must also undertake to recognize how the need for a viable identity in the present shapes our understanding of the past.

Chapter 2, "Teacher as Historian," focuses on my exploration of the life of Edward Isham, a poor white southerner who was hanged in 1860 for the murder he committed under his alias, Hardaway Bone. This memoir of historical research explores what it means for the public school teacher to cross the boundary from transmitter to creator of knowledge. A meditation on embodying both of these roles, this chapter also considers how the present offers a commentary on the past.

Chapter 3, "Teacher as Apostle of Dangerous Memory," asserts that the teacher's role subverts the established order when we go beyond individual stories of a personal identity rooted in the past to seek those narratives that challenge how we have conceived justice, opportunity, and fairness. Rejected is postmodernism's argument that historical narrative merely maintains the existing conditions in our society because it is incapable of offering critical analysis.

Chapter 4, "The Limits of Enlightenment," argues that what we can know is limited by the incompleteness of our views of the past and of ourselves. While acknowledging that ours is a flawed existence, we are saved from tragedy by insisting that we retain the agency needed to change the world. Paradoxically, recognizing our limitations does not remove the burden of acting within them and of attempting to push beyond them in order to effect change. Only by faith in transcending the present can we morally justify our teaching.

The chapters of Part II, "From Theory to Practice," offer the most convincing examples I know which use historical documents (with no claim to exhausting their possibilities or to providing a seamless curriculum guide to United States history) to illuminate the past in ways that allow students to consider issues of individual and societal identity. Each of the chapters, therefore, poses an inquiry into the past that is impelled by the desire to understand who we are.

Chapter 5, "The Past I Have Known," traces the struggle of a young, inexperienced history teacher to survive in a public school classroom. With much of what I had studied and believed to be of value being challenged by students holding priorities different from mine, I found it necessary for the first time (though hardly the last) to demonstrate how studying the past was relevant to living in the present.

Chapter 6, "Fridays Belong to Ned Cobb," continues with the idea of giving voice to one's identity by considering three literary works that testify in moving and sometimes disturbing ways to what it is like to live in a racially divided south: the autobiography of Nate Shaw in Theodore Rosengarten's *All God's Dangers*; the autobiographical novel *A Fool's Errand* by Albion Tourgée; and the inflammatory novels of Thomas Dixon, in particular *The Clansman*.

Chapter 7, "Interpreting the Past with Light and Shadow," turns to the historical documentation provided by photography which has power in our culture to shape identities. Whether considered as personal memento, social document, or captured moment, the photograph gives an immediacy to the past often absent in the written record—an important consideration for the history teacher.

Chapter 8, "Reading Really Old Textbooks," examines passages from textbooks of the common-school era for messages that communicate the values nineteenth-century educators wished to inculcate in their students. Such a careful reading reveals many of the assumptions on which the nation was built while, even more importantly, sensitizing students to the otherwise alien notion that the textbook is more than a repository of inert fact.

Throughout the writing of this book I was unsure what value it would have for anyone else. My fear has been that it was the worst kind of autobiography—ruminative, but not illuminating. Perhaps the best I can do is to show the manner in which I have traveled down a difficult road in the hope that my testimony can be as potent as another's more cogent exhortation.

Notes

[1] Ellen Glasgow, *In This Our Life* (New York: Harcourt Brace and Company, 1941) 8.

[2] Ellen Glasgow, *A Certain Measure: An Interpretation of Prose Fiction* (New York: Harcourt Brace and Company, 1943) 249.

[3] Glasgow, *A Certain Measure* 250.

PART I
Underpinnings

Chapter 1

A Personal Account of Fashioning History

We struggle to arrange the shards of our personal pasts into patterns that help us make sense of who we are. Unlike the pieces of a broken pot, however, our life stories can be ordered in various and plausible arrangements. While the healthiest of us understands that some configurations more closely resemble the facts as a bystander might observe them, we also come to accept that even our most persuasive fashionings are riddled with incompleteness, puzzlement, and paradox. No matter how we try, the patterns will remain fragmentary.

Ludwig van Beethoven offers one particularly vivid, if unconscious, example of an individual attempting to fashion a usable past. In a study informed by Freudian psychoanalytic theory, Maynard Solomon describes this composer as convinced—despite documentation to the contrary which was available to him—that he had been born a year later than was commonly acknowledged, and as unwilling, regardless of how it might reflect upon his mother's reputation, to deny persistent rumors that Johann van Beethoven was not his father. Admiring of the accomplished *Kapellmeister* who was his paternal grandfather, and resentful of the drunken musical mediocrity of his father, Beethoven fantasized about a royal parentage to ease the "matrix of negative feelings" fostered by a painful childhood.[1] Never mind for now the facts which Beethoven ignored in order to build his fantasy; honesty was less important to him than the empowerment he found by disconnecting himself from a past he rejected.

Our knowledge of the past is always incomplete and, more important, selective. Consciously or not, we choose which stories to tell, which means that other stories remain untold. Furthermore, as the example from Beethoven's life demonstrates, the stories we use to mold our identity may rest more on fantasy than on fact. While selection, omission, and distortion are plagues that afflict each of us, they especially vex the historian.

Consider how three sketches drawn from a family genealogy demonstrate the challenges of coming to terms with the past. The three sketches, together with diversions into other branches of the family, make no claim to the authoritativeness most historians hope to bring to their work. Rather than marking destinations, they point down lines of inquiry that may never find permanent resolution.

The first sketch moves us from the Old World to the New World. The destructiveness of the Thirty Years' War (1618–1648) left a German population in tatters and political and ecclesiastical administrations in chaos. While the Treaty of Westphalia ended the religious wars of the Reformation, the Rhine River valley suffered further under the brutally aggressive foreign policy of France's Louis XIV, whose armies swept through the area beginning in 1672 during their assault on the Netherlands. Years of strife helped to deaden the reform spirit of Lutheranism, providing a fertile ground for the multiplicity of Pietists who wished to return Christianity to what they believed were its "experimental, emotional, individual, biblically centered, and ethically minded" origins.[2]

Not surprisingly, the German Pietists, who called themselves Brethren, met with distrust and persecution from civil and church authorities fearful of the mysticism that characterized these radical Protestants. The Brethren who gathered at their "mother church" in the Westphalian town of Schwarzenau eventually determined to emigrate to William Penn's colony of dissenters. In 1729, a large contingent of Brethren arrived in the Germantown, Pennsylvania area to build a community that rested upon their desire to live separate from the ways of the world. Included among the new arrivals were Johann Heinrich Kalkglässer, his wife, and their four children. Within a few years, the family settled along the Conestoga frontier in a commune called Ephrata.[3] Much of his later life remains veiled from us, but, before his death in 1748, Kalkglässer was a respected enough leader to have been appointed to a delegation that explored the sensitive topic of establishing closer ties with Zinzendorf's Moravians.[4] Although Kalkglässer desired to leave at least a portion of his estate to Ephrata, the commune soon afterward began its decline into obscurity.[5]

The thread of this family history is lost for now. Even so, we know that the frontier turmoil of the French and Indian War ended the isolated existence at Ephrata. At the same time, Virginia's Shenandoah Valley began to attract Brethren, Mennonites, and Dunkards.[6] Perhaps, therefore, it was a descendant of Heinrich Kalkglässer who years later came to lease a manufacturing mill on the Shadwell estate of Thomas Jefferson. A man named Colclaser—Jefferson provides no first name, but the 1820 federal census for Albemarle County, Virginia lists one Daniel Coleclaser—is referred to several times in Jefferson's *Farm Book* with entries like this one: "1817. Aug 2 Colclaser says that a man saws & rives the timber & dresses complctely for setting up staves for 250 barrels a day, 17. staves to a barrel."[7] Despite Jefferson's interest in manufacturing and his considerable expenditures on the mill house, dam, and canal, the investment proved a bad one, owing to "poor management, controversies with the lessees, and the constant repairs" the facility required.[8] By the early 1820s, Colclaser had given his part of the lease to Thomas Eston Randolph and disappeared from Jefferson's records. It is unknown whether or not he continued to work in the area as a miller.

Once again a gap appears. Did Colclaser's relatives, like so many before them, use the Shenandoah Valley as a highway to the Carolinas? Perhaps, then, the miller was kin to a Baptist who lived in South Carolina's Edgefield County. The Horn's Creek Baptist Church recorded in 1838 that "Brother William Colclazur having accidentally killed one of his own Negro boys by striking him on the head with a stick, disciplined himself."[9] Although in this instance unspecified, church discipline was "deeply rooted in the evangelical sense of community and in a desire to create a culture rooted in otherworldly compassion."[10] One wonders whether Colclazur was stirred by a half-forgotten memory of the family's earlier devotion to communal life. How he balanced his faith, his slaveholding, and his punishment is unrecorded, but he was restored to the church's fellowship. Whether he continued to prosper as he (or perhaps his father) apparently did at the time of the 1830 federal census—when, aged between fifty and sixty years, William Culclazier was listed as living in a household that included six slaves—is also uncertain, for his name does not appear again in census reports.[11]

Riddling this brief account of a family's history are numerous gaps, silences, and omissions. Even the links between Kalkglässer, Colclaser, and Colclazur (Culclazier) are no more than informed speculation. Suppose, however, that the genealogy was clear; more fundamental concerns about the fashioning of history would remain unaddressed. No woman is named in this lineage, based as it is on paternal ancestry, and so completely do men's surnames dominate antebellum documents that recovering a wife's maiden name poses a challenge. Not surprisingly in a society that severely limited a wife's ability to freely dispose of her property, maintaining a personal identity, not to mention a legal standing separate from her husband's, was a difficult task for a woman.[12]

Court records and governors' papers—sources that are often underutilized—capture the voices of humbler classes of citizens. Legal cases in which women are party dramatically illustrate the difficulty of clearly distinguishing them while at the same time illuminating the bonds between wives and their husbands. In the court records of the 1855 trial of Alvin Preslar for killing his wife, for example, the brutally beaten Esther was not even named (newspaper accounts fill this void). All that can be discerned of her in those records is that she was "a fat woman." Two trials were required before Preslar was convicted of murder, in part because of the defense's arguments that Alvin's drunkenness should be considered a mitigating factor and that Esther was in no immediate danger of losing her life when she fled their cabin and needlessly exposed herself to the damp night air. Ironically, even the status of their hapless children—one of whom, at eighteen years old, was hardly a child—was invoked in a petition to the governor to spare Alvin from the gallows.[13]

Incorporating the stories of women into historical narratives has not been easy. The crudest method of doing so has been to show them heroically performing what had been seen as men's work. The effect can be puzzling for readers unsure of women's roles at the time, as suggested by a photograph caption given in one high school history textbook's tediously detailed chapter on the Civil War: "Women played a variety of crucial roles on both sides during the war. Some women . . . disguised themselves as men and joined the front lines. Others . . . performed important medical tasks."[14] The exceptional does not do much to illustrate the typical, and while the text may acknowledge this fact, its bland, fact-laden paragraphs do more to gloss over than to illuminate the experiences of most women. For the great majority of both free and slave women throughout much of our history, lives exhausted in childbearing and homemaking reflected more of a somber, Hobbesian struggle than a consensual, Lockean arrangement. Women like Abigail Adams, Elizabeth Cady Stanton, and Ida B. Wells, who both entered and challenged male domains, should rightfully come into the pantheon of American luminaries, but they may help us comprehend the lives of their obscure cohorts only by negative example. "[I]f the vindication of women depends on the discovery of an adequate supply of forgotten writers and power-brokers," Robert Darnton has asked, "what is to be done if the numbers turn out to be disappointing?"[15]

What is to be done, as Darnton acknowledged, is to examine how womanhood has been understood across the ages. As with Esther Preslar, glimpsed through the transcript of a murder trial, we see a striking image that nevertheless easily escapes us, like the silvery likeness of a daguerreotype. Continuing to search court records we also realize that Esther kept grim company with other women whose partially documented lives (and deaths) help describe the status of their sex. Samuel Parker Perry, for example, not content with merely degrading his spouse by forcing her to sleep on the floor with a quilt while he occupied a feather bed, murdered his wife Caroline—who was described as "idiotic" in the 1850 federal census—by striking her head with an axe and then throwing her down a well.[16] "Damn you, it's nothing to you if I kill her," Perry snarled at a woman neighbor who dared to interfere in an earlier beating; and it is very likely that the cause of Caroline's derangement had much to do with Samuel's treatment of her, which also included his openly keeping a mistress.[17] Like Alvin Preslar, Samuel Parker Perry was hanged for his crime, but not before the governor of North Carolina reviewed petitions signed by individuals—including jurors—who thought that the defendant should be pardoned.[18] While individual men might be condemned by the law, society empathized with a husband's disciplining of his wife and, in the event of her death, mitigating factors like drunkenness. To be sure, as Victoria Bynum has demonstrated, there were limits to the brutality communities were willing to accept; to be fair, both Preslar and Perry were condemned by their peers. Inescapable in a patriarchal society, however, was the fact that violence and intoxication were male domains just as surely as was the management of property, marriage, and divorce.[19]

A richer history results from acknowledging the complexity of women's life in the antebellum South—where women were alternately sainted and disciplined—than from a frustrating search for evidence of "great women" to match with "great men" in a culture which tightly circumscribed feminine roles. At the same time, the temptation to view southern women simply as hapless victims robs them of their humanity just as much as trying to evaluate them by a man's measure of success. It also illustrates an unwillingness to search beyond the traditional sources—the political and literary documents of a man's public world—and to consider conceptualizations of history that do not denigrate the common and the private.

If a woman's world was more domestic and less public than a man's and therefore less likely to have been documented, it was nevertheless vibrant and resourceful in preserving a sense of family and community, a theme that has especially attracted the attention of historians of the South. "Family, kin, and neighbors defined the boundaries of the social world in the countryside," write the authors of *Like a Family: The Making of a Southern Cotton Mill World*.[20] The authors, whose collection of oral histories from Piedmont mill town families comprises the core of the work's documentation, conclude that families working in the booming cotton mills of the New South preserved a sense of community despite their dislocation from the land and that this owes to the mixture of cooperation and resistance which characterized their response to the factory system's paternalism. Because families, and not simply individuals, took up "public work" in the cotton mills, women did much to preserve community values of sustenance that had previously served families struggling to survive the dislocations wrought by the rise of white tenantry, the grip of the lien system, and the decline of cotton prices. The near past allows historians to interview its participants. For earlier generations such knowledge is frequently too ephemeral to have been preserved deliberately, although its traces may be discerned indirectly through folklore, custom, or literature.[21]

Recovering the voices of women—whether through oral histories, diaries, letters, and memoirs, or through census reports and court records—remains less of a challenge than thinking of history in terms of family and community instead of in terms of individuals. Economic questions can be framed by examining household production as well as the dynamics between the planter and the market. In this way, slave culture becomes as important as slave production; the roles of faith and religion reemerge as central concerns for understanding how a life was lived; honor and virtue explain as much about past life as politics and economics; the common receives attention just as the extraordinary does. In short, life in the past more closely resembles life in the present, with its complex web of relationships and spheres of action.

The dramas of murderous crime, courtroom testimony, and earnest petitioning illustrate the tensions that exist beneath a society's outward consensus. These incidents should not, however, be mistaken for representing how most southerners lived, no matter their gender, color, or status. More typical of the period was the life of Sarah, wife of Nathan Wesley Culclasure, who faced the daunting task of surviving a man's work. Nathan and Sarah Culclasure—aged twenty-six and twenty-eight, respectively—owned $3,000 of real estate and $4,000 of personal property, according to the 1860 federal census.[22] Their substantial holdings near St. Matthews, South Carolina included six slaves.[23] None of the couple's three sons were old enough to contribute to the family's labor. Even so, Nathan enlisted, perhaps through conscription, in the Confederate army in November 1863.[24] Hospitalized with a fever in the spring of 1864 and then taken prisoner in October at Strasburg, Virginia (site of German settlements in the Shenandoah Valley a century earlier), the war was surely a trying experience for him and his family.

Nathan lived long enough after he returned from the war to father three more children, two daughters and a son. He died shortly before the taking of the 1870 census, however, because the thirty-nine-year-old Sarah was listed that year as head of the household.[25] The two eldest boys—Daniel, aged fourteen years, and Nathan, aged twelve years—were described as farm laborers. The farm was valued at only $1,000 and Sarah's personal property was listed at a mere $200. Whether the freedmen who once served the family continued to work on the farm or had struck out on their own is unknown. Either way, their lives, just as the lives of their former owners, had been changed profoundly.

A family history might easily overlook Sarah and concentrate instead on the bloodline of her children. Sarah, however, offers a story worth attempting to recover. Amidst the devastation of the region and the dislocation of her own life, how did Sarah sustain her family, especially in a time of declining land values, rising taxes, and transformed relations with black labor? Perhaps, as the wife of a slaveholding farmer, she possessed the knowledge and fortitude to undertake the work of her now-dead husband.[26] Certainly her children, who continued to live in the area after 1880 when she last appeared in a census report, came of age early. In any event, her story was shared by other women who lived through the era of Reconstruction without the husbands of their youth.[27]

There are other, more difficult to acknowledge omissions in this family genealogy. William Colclazur beating a slave to death points to a particularly haunting part of our nation's history. So, too, does the life of another member of that family, David Culclasure—not the David of Orange Parish, South Carolina, who in 1840 owned twenty-eight slaves, but an individual with the same name who lived most of his life after the Civil War.[28] The latter-day David Culclasure was sixty years old in 1910.[29] He farmed in the same Orangeburg County, South Carolina as others with the same surname. He, however, was black. Although he could read, his wife Lillian, to whom he had been married for thirty-eight years, could not. Together with their daughter Leila (who had fifteen living children herself), two youthful grandchildren (who may have been Leila's children), and a son also named David and his wife of six years, the family worked land they did not own. All the children and grandchildren listed were literate, but David was old enough to have been born a slave about 1850.

An Orangeburg District tax list of 1851 shows the estate of David Culclasure, the slaveholder, possessing 1,500 acres of land and fifteen slaves (for which the estate was assessed $9.45).[30] The old man was about eighty when he died in 1846, not long before the birth of David Culclasure, the slave. Whether any connection existed between these two individuals who lived close to each other and shared a common given name and an uncommon surname is unclear, although the question of whether the black Culclasure was a member of the same family is inescapable. Quite apart from the blood ties that bound many slaves to their masters, the two men—one white and the other black—were joined to each other by a system that degraded both of them in different ways.

Put another way, the question of relation bears on the present: Do the sins of the past inextricably tie us together in the present? We fear the answer, not simply from the dread of discovering that we share taboo blood lines, but because we may find we are responsible. The past does not fasten guilt upon the present so much as it presses responsibility for ensuring that we do not, within our limited capabilities, further its evils. After all, history is our creation, used to understand the past, and we are responsible to each other for choosing to tell some stories while leaving others, whether out of ignorance or design, untold. To deny this responsibility is to deny our shared humanity. We should not be surprised when we discover that those who have felt excluded from history also believe that it has nothing to say to the present. Resentful of authority unjustly wielded, much of the present generation resents the slightest imputation that anyone has anything important to tell it.

How, then, are the two David Culclasures—white and

black—to be reconciled with one another? One is struck by how they are presented in census reports: the former attached to the figures that described his holdings and the latter joined to the names of the three generations who lived in his household (to be fair, a function of the different census formats, but also an occasion for wonder). Their stories, as well as they can be recovered, must be recognized as equally valid and, most essentially, as related. Despite the enmity that may have existed between them, each of their lives was defined by the other's inescapable presence.[31] The importance of their stories lies less in narrow questions of labor and production than in how a sense of humanity was preserved in the presence of evil.

No southerner can make sense of his or her history without reference to others who, though different, are connected. Pretending otherwise represents a seduction of the present to a distorted view of the past; a seduction because it pretends that a seamless, comfortable, half-story faithfully reflects our paradoxical, quirky, and sometimes hurtful selves. If we cannot find ourselves in the past it is as if our existence is denied. To deny the complexities of our existence is more than misleading; the people we omit are wronged.

In an era when the old middle class guarantees of steady employment and a secure family have evaporated, we long for stability yet hardly have the patience to listen to stories that are not our own, fearful they will somehow further diminish our significance. Instead, we exhaust ourselves with contests over symbols like the Confederate flag. As an uneven prosperity heightens the disparity between city and countryside, affluent and marginal, well-educated and poorly schooled, white southerners who once were confident of their superiority strive to preserve their identity by talking of heritage, while black southerners tire of being expected to patiently bear the latent hostility embedded in the memory of a secession movement that promised to constitutionally guarantee slavery's permanence. As a symbol, the Battle Flag is only the outward manifestation of the contest for historical memory, testimony to how we rely on the past in order to understand who we are. Were we more accepting of the paradox winding through our history that links slavery and freedom, we might also be more accepting of the need both sides feel to find meaning for themselves in a history that cannot help but be shared. (Maintaining a state identity, however, that is rooted more in resistance to the Civil Rights movement of the 1950s—when the stars and cross appeared on state flags—than in the Civil War is another question. As Howard Zinn has argued, "we must not accept the memory of states as our own. Nations are not communities and never have been."[32])

So uncertain are we of our identity that even when we do discover our links with the past we continue to hope for further validation. How important is it to say, for example, that the modest Daniel Colclaser worked for the everlasting Thomas Jefferson? Certainly we would know much less about him if not for Jefferson's correspondence. At the same time, Colclaser seems to grow in significance because of his association with Jefferson, which says more about the present's need for status than it does about what the miller might have thought. Singled out as individuals, Jefferson's merit in deserving historical scholarship would outweigh Colclaser's. After all, we live in a nation that has enshrined much of his political thinking. We also live in a nation, however, that was built through the work of countless anonymous laborers. Jefferson could not enjoy his life as a gentleman farmer without the efforts of his workers, many of whom did not experience freedom. Basing history solely on the studies of individuals makes it easy to value some over others. In contrast, tracing the relationship between employer and employee (master and slave, or husband and wife) points us to a history in which the workings of a community's relationships are as important as the individuals in those relationships.

Of the family members earlier described, Heinrich Kalkglässer remains the most enigmatic, and not simply because of his remoteness in time. While Kalkglässer clearly lived in a community with his peers, he also lived in a setting so different from any we inhabit that it is nearly incomprehensible. The Ephrata commune in which he and his family lived, shunning as it did the temptations of greater spiritual influence and a prosperous material existence, lacked the flexibility to survive as a distinctive society beyond the early nineteenth century.[33] At Ephrata, the individual acted only within the strict confines of the community, which was dedicated to preserving a vision of transcendent truth from the wiles of a hostile world. Missionary activities notwithstanding, the commune did not survive in a land that was more attuned to the pragmatism of Benjamin Franklin's Poor Richard than to the Brethren tracts his press also printed.

As the world's first "modern" nation, dedicated to the principle that the individual possesses rights derived from nature, the

United States, ironically, has provided both the opportunity for communal enterprises like Ephrata and the virtual guarantee of their impermanence. Neither intense individuality nor the close atmosphere of communal living remain fresh in the other's company. The decision of Heinrich Kalkglässer's descendants, however, to leave Ephrata for new settlements that were not imbued with the founding generation's sense of mission, carried its own risks. Shorn of a common sense of purpose and place within a close-knit community, the new settlers were left to struggle on their own. While the industrialization of both manufacturing and agriculture were required to accelerate and dramatize the plight of individuals competing within vast impersonal markets, Alexis de Tocqueville observed as early as the 1830s the importance of "the art of association" in maintaining a civil society.[34] The Ephrata commune—however otherworldly its existence may appear to a less mystical, more rational audience—posed a tension familiar to contemporary society: how identity is created within community and, conversely, maintained apart from it.[35]

Unlike us, the Ephrata settlers counted on the aid of a God who both joined together and separately identified. The commune's belief that God's spirit could be felt within each individual, calling the faithful to forsake the worldly for the heavenly, requires a transcendence of self-interest we find impossible to make. (Even the call for rebirth made by our culture's evangelical Protestantism is pitched in terms of a self-interest that is as palpable as it is pragmatic. The new believer hopes both to save himself from eternal damnation and to find himself blessed in this life as well.) Our society's brave assertion of democratic truths—in which more recently we also have largely lost faith—remains our closest collective approach to transcendence. Even so, the individualism which has grown out of our assertion of rights has led us down so many separate and lonely paths that we fear entangling ourselves in thickets of economic hardship and personal alienation more than we hope to pursue happiness.

The preaching of cracked old certainties about work, family, and moral values in strident and masculine voices sounds the depths of our insecurity. In our fear of the future, we mistakenly try to cling to a past too reified to sustain us. History becomes a burden when we believe that its experience can be transferred intact to the present. Our lives are our own. While their potentialities are sometimes limited by the past's influence, they cannot be lived as if the only possibilities are the old ones.

In a study that has attempted to link the study of history with modernism, Marshall Berman asserts that "remembering the modernisms of the nineteenth century can give us vision and courage to create the modernism of the twenty-first."[36] Berman thereby implicitly challenges the notion of history marching to the drumbeat of progress by suggesting that, because our knowledge is so fragmentary, we can learn from how past generations coped with the modern era's turmoil. Berman's emphasis that the past is necessary for realizing meaning in the present is corollary to the idea that the present shapes our view of the past. The old certainties may continue to teach and inspire, but they will not substitute for the striving required of us to determine their validity for today. Should we choose now to abandon the upkeep of a civic culture in which we can find common ground without surrendering our differences, our quest for personal meaning also will be frustrated. The paradox is inescapable: Only in the security of community can individual identity be realized. Conversely, without the liberty to fashion an identity richly textured in historical understanding, the secure community we long for will be unrealized.

Despite our pragmatic reputation, the peoples of this nation have espoused transcendent principles that serve, when we allow them, to unite us. Even with its gaps and omissions, the personal histories related earlier embody these principles: Heinrich Kalkglässer's flight from religious persecution; Daniel Colclaser's struggle to make viable an economic undertaking; William Colclazur's awareness of his complicity with evil and the limits to his authority. Furthermore, each of these individual accounts exists only in relation to a broader social context, whether the context be the individual living within a religious commune, the affairs linking the great to the forgotten man, or the relations binding together the free and the enslaved. The pieces of our stories are incomplete fragments, except when they are joined with the pieces of others' stories.

Enabling each individual to find himself or herself in the past may pain us, especially if, for example, we discover that the descendants of the white David Culclasure have fared better than the ones of the black David Culclasure for no better reason than the color of their skin. We should be careful, however, to remember that what we see in the past is shaped by the concerns of the present. While we may be required to live with the consequences of past wrongs, we distort the past by expecting it to conform to our present values. Herein lies another paradox: While the history we fashion reflects our points of view, the past cannot be condemned for failing to share, or even recognize, our sensibilities. Instead, what is worthy of our execration is the use of history to condemn those of the present generation. The absence of people we have deemed unworthy of study in our historical accounts should not blind us to how history-telling involves chosen ways of perceiving the past, ways that may be rooted in our biases and prejudices.

In this sense, history is as much about the present as it is about the past. The author's family account herein related attempted to emphasize the gaps and omissions, the societal context, and the unsung and forgotten, out of the belief that these elements are the ones most lacking in the presentation of history to young people today. It is more than a desire to enliven the curriculum that is at issue. Of greater concern is the students' sense that they are being denied their identity by being disconnected from their past. The stories we come to tell, and listen to, may be dark, but they are redeemed with the dignity that humanity maintains even as it displays its greatest indignities.

Ultimately, the fragments of a family's story speak to the identity of the author just as it does to his ancestors. This account represents an author's desire to sense rootedness, ponder faith, find significance, and weigh guilt. The messages teased from the story are moral because they reflect a conviction that our existence is understood by contemplating our inescapably lonely struggle for validation as we yearn for closeness with others. Paradoxes like this one, in turn, point to an underlying belief that we best grasp life by balancing an awareness of its limitations with a faith in its potentialities. Such an attitude, asserts Christopher Lasch, embodies a hope that rests not on the optimist's belief in future progress but on confidence in a past which shows "that trust is never completely misplaced, even though it is never completely justified either and therefore destined inevitably to disappointments."[37]

We struggle with the incompleteness of our knowledge but, instead of despairing, we wonder at the miracle of creativity that makes history a birthright for each of us. Even so, the awareness of our dependence upon others fosters a humility about our ability to faithfully capture all of the past's complexities. In telling our stories, we find that some are more convincing than others because they more carefully maintain historical integrity. We cannot succumb to the corrosive fancy that insisting on fidelity to standards of historical research means no more than furthering the oppression of the status quo. How our stories are told becomes as important as which ones we choose to hear.

Notes

[1] Maynard Solomon, *Beethoven* (New York: Schirmer Books, 1977) 22.

[2] Donald F. Durnbaugh, *The Believers' Church: The History and Character of Radical Protestantism* (New York: Macmillan, 1968) 119.

[3] The Ephrata settlement is notable especially for its spiritual music and Frakturschriften art. In addition, Conrad Beissel, Ephrata's charismatic founder, provided the subject for Thomas Mann's *Doctor Faustus* (1948). The settlement has been preserved as a Pennsylvania state park. See E. G. Alderfer, *The Ephrata Commune: An Early American Counterculture* (Pittsburgh: University of Pittsburgh Press, 1985).

[4] Alderfer 80.

[5] *Collections of the Genealogical Society of Pennsylvania: Abstracts of Lancaster County, Pennsylvania, Wills, 1721–1820*, vol. 24.

[6] Alderfer 135–44.

[7] Daniel Coleclaser is described as between twenty-six and forty-five years old and employed in manufactures. His household also included a woman of the same age span—presumably his wife—and a young female slave. See Fourth Census, 1820: Albemarle County, Virginia, Population Schedule. The Jefferson quote is from Edwin Morris Betts, ed., *Thomas Jefferson's Farm Book* (Charlottesville: University Press of Virginia, 1987) 123.

[8] Betts 341–2.

[9] Quoted in Orville Vernon Burton, *In My Father's House Are Many Mansions: Family and Community in Edgefield, South Carolina* (Chapel Hill: University of North Carolina Press, 1985) 59.

[10] Robert M. Calhoon, *Evangelicals and Conservatives in the Early South, 1740–1861* (Columbia: University of South Carolina Press, 1988) 111.

[11] Fifth Census, 1830: Edgefield County, South Carolina, Population Schedule. In addition to William Culclazier, the household included a white female, aged forty to fifty years, a white male, aged fifteen to twenty years, and a white female, aged fifteen to twenty years. Three male slaves were listed as aged under ten years, twenty to twenty-four years, and twenty-four to thirty-six years. Three female slaves were also listed, one in each of the same age spans. According to her obituary, wife Elizabeth [née?] Culclazer was born May 28, 1787. She joined Horn's Creek Baptist Church in 1809 and married William on February 6, 1810. She died at age sixty-two on October 3, 1848. The obituary mentions only her surviving husband and daughter. On February 13, 1853, William Culclazier married Mary Ann Cartledge. Because William Culclazier's wedding dates are so widely separated, two individuals with the same name are possible. See Carlee T. McClendon, comp., *Edgefield Death Notices and Cemetery Records* (Columbia, S.C.: Hive Press, 1977) 71, 248 and *Edgefield Marriage Records, Edgefield, South Carolina: From the Late Eighteenth Century up through 1870* (Columbia, S.C.: R. L. Bryan, 1970) 44. The 1860 census shows Mrs. M. Culclazier, aged forty-five years, living in the same county as a farmer (owning $5,000 in real estate and $14,000 in personal property) with her five-year-old son William J., her brother Joseph Cartledge, and sister-in-law Betsy. Eighth Census, 1860: Edgefield County, South Carolina, Population Schedule.

[12] Victoria E. Bynum, *Unruly Women: The Politics of Social and Sexual Control in the Old South* (Chapel Hill: University of North Carolina Press, 1992) 64–5.

[13] Bynum 82–83 and Scott P. Culclasure, "Edward Isham and Criminal Justice for the Poor White in Antebellum North Carolina," *Journal of Southern Legal History* III (1994): 80–83. That a group of "ladies" was willing to add their names to the petitions calling for Preslar's pardon suggests their evangelical role of agents seeking the mercy of the governor. See petitions and correspondence dated December 15, 20, and 22, 1856, Governors Papers, 141 and Governors Letter Books, 43: 635, 639, 642–5, 651, North Carolina State Archives. See also Charles C. Bolton and Scott P. Culclasure, eds., *The Confessions of Edward Isham: A Poor White Life of the Old South* (Athens, Georgia: University of Georgia Press, 1998).

[14] The example is taken from one of the more sophisticated history textbooks used in high schools. See Carol Berkin et al., *American Voices: A History of the United States* (Glenview, Illinois: Scott, Foresman and Company, 1992) 230–1. A happy exception that proves the rule is Joy Hakim's *A History of US* (New York: Oxford University Press, 2d ed., 1999), a ten-volume history that is comprehensive, sophisticated, and refuses to talk down to its audience. Hakim's work is reviewed by Alexander Stille in the context of other, more dismal history textbooks in "The Betrayal of History," *The New York Review of Books* 11 June 1998: 15.

[15] Robert Darnton, "Cherchez la Femme," rev. of *Monsieur d'Eon Is a Woman: A Tale of Political Intrigue and Sexual Masquerade*, by Gary Kates, *The New York Review of Books* 10 August 1995: 22.

[16] Perry is listed in the 1850 census as a farmer aged thirty-five years and owning $1,000 worth of real estate. Caroline was aged thirty-six years. The household also included Mary, aged nine years, and Mary Lasiter, aged thirty-one years. Polly Lassiter was identified in court testimony as having assumed the position of mistress of the household after the onset of Caroline's mental illness. Seventh Census of the United States, 1850: Wake County, North Carolina, Population Schedule. The case is reported in State v. Samuel P. Perry, 44 N.C. 330 (1853). Testimony from the trial, which does not survive in court records, was printed in "The State vs. Parker Perry," *North Carolina Standard* (Raleigh), April 20, 1853.

[17] "The State vs. Parker Perry," *North Carolina Standard* (Raleigh), April 20, 1853. The newspaper concluded that "No verdict of the Jury was ever more just than the one rendered in this case."

[18] September [ ], 28, and October 14, 1853, Governors Papers, 134 and October 14, 1853, Governors Letter Books, 41: 140–1, North Carolina State Archives. See also Culclasure, "Edward Isham" 81, 85 and Bolton and Culclasure, *The Confessions of Edward Isham.*

[19] The author is indebted to Victoria E. Bynum for emphasizing how drunkenness was a masculine prerogative and, therefore, a mitigating factor that was gendered. See also Bynum 83.

[20] Jacquelyn Dowd Hall, James Leloudis, Robert Korstad, Mary Murphy, Lu Ann Jones, and Christopher B. Daly, *Like a Family: The Making of a Southern Cotton Mill World* (Chapel Hill: University of North Carolina Press, 1987) 23.

[21] Two recent examples of how historians can tease meaning out of the obscure include E. P. Thompson, *Customs in Common: Studies in Traditional Popular Culture* (New York: The New Press, 1991) and Robert Darnton, *The Forbidden Best-Sellers of Pre-Revolutionary France* (New York: W. W. Norton, 1995). While Thompson focuses on the culture of English working people in the eighteenth century, Darnton explores how French public opinion was formulated and articulated through censored but surreptitiously popular works of literature.

[22] Eighth Census: 1860, Orangeburg County, South Carolina, Population Schedule.

[23] Eighth Census: 1860, Orangeburg County, South Carolina, Slave Schedule. Considered as property rather than persons, enslaved people were listed on a separate schedule in the 1860 census by age, gender, and race (black or mulatto). The six slaves of Culclasure's estate consisted of three black females, aged seventy, fourteen, and seven years, and three black males, aged thirty-five, twelve, and twelve years.

[24] Confederate Military Service Records, National Archives, Washington, D.C.

[25] Ninth Census, 1870: Orangeburg County, South Carolina, Population Schedule.

[26] That white women who were listed in postwar censuses as the head of household were likely to be relatively old, widowed, and rarely with very small children is shown in Burton 284–7.

[27] For an example of how Reconstruction's stresses affected the landowning status of Rosetta Hurley of Montgomery County, North Carolina, see Bynum 152–4. Of yeoman stock and an unmarried mother, Hurley's fate was likely more extreme than that which Sarah Culclasure faced. The 1880 census described Sarah as a widowed farmer with four children still living at home. Two sons—Charles, the twenty-year-old, and Francis, the twelve-year-old—were farm laborers. Although the sixteen-year-old Lizzie had attended school, Francis and twelve-year-old Marion were listed as illiterate. Tenth Census: 1880, Orangeburg County, South Carolina, Population Schedule.

[28] Sixth Census: 1840, Orangeburg County, South Carolina, Population Schedule.

[29] Thirteenth Census: 1910, Orangeburg County, South Carolina, Population Schedule.

[30] "1851 Orangeburg District Tax List," *The South Carolina Magazine of Ancestral Research* VII (1979): 18.

[31] On the gathering of families, black and white, "that would shatter a century of silence" about life on a North Carolina plantation, see Dorothy Spruill Redford, *Somerset Homecoming: Recovering a Lost Heritage* (New York: Anchor Books Doubleday, 1988) 205–37. For a personal recollection of the labryrinthine relationships between whites and blacks in a North Carolina village of the 1950s, see Melton A. McLaurin, *Separate Pasts: Growing Up White in the Segregated South*

(Athens, Georgia: University of Georgia Press, 1987). Against the silence of his white family, Edward Ball tells of a past that depended on the labor of slaves in *Slaves in the Family* (New York: Farrar Straus & Giroux, 1998).

[32] Howard Zinn, *A People's History of the United States, 1492–Present*, rev. ed. (New York: HarperPerennial, 1995) 9.

[33] Alderfer 77, 83.

[34] Alexis de Tocqueville, *Democracy in America*, trans. George Lawrence, ed. J. P. Mayer (New York: Anchor Books, 1969) 517. De Tocqueville was referring to associations that were intellectual and moral rather than political and economic. Churches, hospitals, prisons, and schools were among the associations that attracted his attention. The effect of capitalist agriculture on freeholding production in the post–Civil War South has been an important theme in many recent studies, including Steven Hahn, *The Roots of Southern Populism; Yeoman Farmers and the Transformation of the Georgia Upcountry, 1850–1890* (New York: Oxford University Press, 1983); Steven Hahn and Jonathan Prude, eds., *The Countryside in the Age of Capitalist Transformation: Essays in the Social History of Rural America* (Chapel Hill: University of North Carolina Press, 1985); and Allen Tullos, *Habits of Industry: White Culture and the Transformation of the Carolina Piedmont* (Chapel Hill: University of North Carolina Press, 1989). A valuable summary of recent scholarship on the subject appears in Edward L. Ayers, *The Promise of the New South: Life After Reconstruction* (New York: Oxford University Press, 1992).

[35] That small, tightly knit, and isolated communities still flourish (apart from the widely publicized paranoia of religious cults and the militia movement) is evident in a recent account of residents of the privately maintained Bear Creek community near Seattle, Washington. At Bear Creek, the "public" space of streets and parks are available only to members of the community. As the houses at Bear Creek are in the $300,000 to $600,000 price range, Seattle leaders worry that affluent voters in this community will choose not to support bond measures designed to improve public facilities in Seattle. See Timothy Egan, "Many Seek Security in Private Communities," *The New York Times* 3 September 1995: A1. Whether private communities are united by more than a desire to flee a world peopled with differences is unclear, but the characteristic they embody of maintaining an identity in an insecure environment drives the fears of many more individuals than those who can afford to live in them.

[36] Marshall Berman, *All That Is Solid Melts Into Air: The Experience of Modernity* (New York: Simon and Schuster, 1982) 36. Berman's belief that modernism leaves us "psychically naked" (129) appears to underemphasize the difficulty of

leaving the past behind. The proposition that human possibilities for remaking the world are unlimited points to the hubris that has plagued modernity and the victims of its gulags, killing fields, and concentration camps.

[37] Christopher Lasch, *The True and Only Heaven: Progress and Its Critics* (New York: W. W. Norton & Company, 1991) 80–1.

Chapter 2

Teacher as Historian

When he was hanged for the murder of James Cornelius in May 1860, few people would have mourned the fate of Edward Isham, or "Hardaway Bone," as he was called by those who knew him in North Carolina. His mother lived too far away—in Chattanooga, Tennessee—to have comforted him, had she even known of her son's fate. Mandy Lesley [Lasley], whom Isham had taken for his wife, had died a year earlier soon after she had given birth to their child. The infant was living with William and Susan Reed [Reid], who knew Isham well enough to have testified at his trial as to his murderous language shortly before the fatal assault. Although he had successfully fled the Catawba County farm where the killing occurred, Isham was quickly tracked down and arrested in the Tennessee mountains, his pursuers no doubt spurred by Austin Cornelius' widely advertised reward of $500 for the arrest of his brother's murderer. The laborers and farmers who had crossed Isham—like the man named Clarke, whose fighting at the time of the August 1858 election resulted in an indictment against Isham for assault and battery; or Washington Sherrill, whose knife served as the murder weapon after Isham had exchanged it for his own worthless one—were likely glad to see such a rival and hothead removed from the scene. For a settled agricultural community more dependent on stability than the rough-and-tumble gold mining region of Georgia where Isham had spent much of his younger life, Hardaway Bone's hanging must have been a relief.[1]

How ironic that someone who made as much noise as Edward Isham was so quickly and completely forgotten. His death excited nowhere as much excitement as had Cornelius', whose gravestone continues to stand long after Isham's grave, presumably unmarked, was lost. The fury of Isham's actions was overtaken by the infinitely greater whirlwind sown at places like Harpers Ferry, raided in the month of Isham's trial. As heinous as his crime was, it could not command from his countrymen the same attention as the battlefield casualty lists newspapers soon were required to print.

Documents describing Isham soon faded from view. The court

book in which Isham's case was minuted under his alias came to be filled with other cases, filed in an out-of-the-way courthouse, and forgotten. Isham's self-told account of his life had been written by his court-appointed lawyer into a notebook which, although preserved, was neglected soon afterward, just as the lawyer himself began to look further afield than the local superior court for a career in state politics.

Historians also turned to topics they considered more promising. The poor were with them always, but the planter had seemingly disappeared, leaving behind visible traces of his existence with which to excite historical inquiry. Simple people lived simple, common lives, with endless cycles of work, marriage, and death, punctuated by inane acts of violence after which commonplace lawyers provided token defenses in which neither they nor any one else in authority much believed. Transient came to mean transparent, unlettered meant unimportant. For historians more interested in the transformative, ordinary life—when it was studied at all—was subjected to a scientism that talked more of group behavior than of individual lives.[2]

The poor, transient, and violent Edward Isham, however, captures our imagination because he personifies what William Faulkner described as "elapsed and yet-elapsing time."[3] Isham's elapsed time challenges the historian to interpret the rare documentation of this individual's life within a cultural context that is now gone. Appreciation of Isham's significance comes from a variety of newer historical studies that counter the postmodernist assertion that narrative is incompatible with critical thinking. These studies focus on the ways in which society has perceived poor white southerners; the significance of violence for people living in a culture saturated with it; the substratum of cultural meaning revealed by an obscure event like the murder of a substantial farmer.[4] The yet-elapsing time reminds the teacher how human alienation and suffering is evident in settings that transcend specific cultural contexts, linking present with past. Witnessing the cruelties inflicted upon our children, in ways that are sometimes casual and removed and occasionally intimate and brutal, also sensitizes a teacher to be receptive to the account of a long-dead individual like Edward Isham.

While the historian meets the challenge of recovering a historical story, the teacher is confronted with the task of understanding how knowledge is defined and then transmitted to the next generation. The roles of historian and teacher have tended toward separation, even isolation, from each other, resulting in learning that is shorn of the creativity and imagination within each of us. The teacher as historian has the opportunity to bring students into the creative process that fashioning history requires—in spite of the frustration of being expected simultaneously to demonstrate scholarly competence to academia and educational relevance to public school administration. Involving students serves a purpose larger than illuminating a historian's work. Teachers neglect—at society's peril—their encouragement of young people's power to shape and validate knowledge. As a culture, we choose which stories we tell and decide how other people should be appreciated. To pretend that knowledge is static and transmittable without being transmutable denies a trait we share in our common humanity: to identify who we are and make sense for ourselves of the world we have inherited.

I could have articulated few of these thoughts when I first encountered Edward Isham, but the ways in which I came to know this historical figure speak to both the past and present. Walking one afternoon along a Raleigh, North Carolina street that led past the Victorian houses of an earlier generation's magnates and politicians—houses whose sagging balustrades and crabgrass lawns heightened a feeling of time's memories slipping away—I wondered if I could enter the State Archives a few blocks ahead of me and capture a sense of the past by calling for some historical document to examine. Without fully comprehending it at the time, I was already thinking toward two ends: showing to myself that even as a teacher I could engage in the historian's creation of knowledge, and demonstrating to my students that the past's secrets could be revealed by anyone with an interest in doing so. Only much later would I be required to confront the realization that teachers were not supposed to behave in this fashion.

Choosing where to begin my historical inquiry was simple: I would peruse the papers of a lawyer who would have felt at home in houses like the ones lining that capital city street. David Schenck (1835–1902) practiced law as a young man, using his profession to make an entry into state politics at the time of the Civil War. To me, however, Schenck was best known for what he had done years afterward. Pursuing a passion for the history of the Revolution in the South, Schenck organized the Guilford Battleground Company in 1887; purchased neglected farmland with the money he raised through this joint-stock company; and established a memorial park that was destined, a few years after his death, to become the first national park to commemorate a Revolutionary War battleground.

My coming of age included working under the engraved gaze of Judge Schenck at the visitor center of what was by then classified as a national military park. The story of the park's establishment, as Schenck related it in his 1893 account, *A Memorial Volume of the Guilford Battle Ground Company*, was both familiar and intriguing, especially when I tried to grasp how the park had changed over the years of its existence and to decide whether it bore much resemblance to the fields and woods the soldiers of Greene and Cornwallis and the area's Quaker and Presbyterian settlers knew in 1781.[5] Surely, being a writer, David Schenck had left a collection of papers residing in a depository like the State Archives, ready to be tapped for forgotten insights.

We limit our learning when we fail to hope for the serendipitous. Even so, no amount of readiness for the unexpected could have prepared me for what I found in the single box of Schenck papers.[6] The discovery of Edward Isham pushed aside thoughts of the battleground, even though the young lawyer's notebook that contained the twenty-seven pages of manuscript that recorded Isham's story defied immediate comprehension. Who was the man whose voice sounded so clear on the pages written in Schenck's hand? As I began to pursue this question, a second one arose which still eludes an answer: Why had David Schenck, embodying as he did Victorian virtues of hard work, sobriety, and a pious regard for family, preserved the story of a man whose violence and apparent shiftlessness marked him for trouble?[7]

For some time I remained unsure of what to do with this account which ended with a cryptic note penciled at the bottom of the last page: "Hanged 25 May 1860." Although I lacked a detailed knowledge of the historiography of the antebellum South, particularly the research reported in the profession's journals, I could not but believe that I would have heard of this man before now, considering how vividly he both embodied and repelled stereotypes of southern life. Here was an illiterate transient who nevertheless told his story with clarity and persuasion. Here was a man who possessed a wide range of labor skills, even though he was poor. Here was a bully who fashioned his story around a framework of unrelenting violence, yet whose voice sounded curiously dispassionate, relating without rancor the string of fights that had comprised his life. In short, here was someone who reflected in many ways the flat image of "po' white trash," but whose life also reminded me of the three-dimensional existence of students I had known. Was it possible that this life was unknown to historians, and, if so, what was I going to do about it?

These thoughts were pushed into the background, however, by the more immediate problem of transcribing the document by hand—the photocopying of a bound notebook being prohibitively expensive—and then typing out a transcript I could use for future research. As much time as this enterprise consumed, even more time was spent on the systematic reading and reflection needed to make the document mean anything. Slowly, Isham came to possess for me a life that had left its mark in census reports, trial records, newspapers, Schenck's diary, and state supreme court reports. The dilettantism that characterized this aspect of my work still awaited the grace of time brought by a research grant before it could be transformed into something approaching what a professional historian might accomplish. Joining the teacher with the historian required more effort, I came to realize, than what was possible, at least by me, in a daily existence in the public schools. This lesson was unsettling. While one individual might struggle with a measure of success against the demands made by work within a technocratic-industrial system of education, there was little hope that many other teachers would similarly be able to engage in learning more fundamental than what was required for the daily lesson plan.

As vital as having the necessary time for study and reflection was, I also needed a historian's model for how Isham's life might be presented to the public. No grand political, military, or diplomatic history could help. Social histories too often reduced individuals to the playthings of historical forces beyond their comprehension, much less control. Quantitative research only diminished the importance of any one individual. In short, I did not know how Isham could be understood within the confines historians had drawn for what constituted acceptable history. Although I continued to believe that my overall assessment of the historical profession was accurate, the feeling that there was no appropriate social history to which I could turn was more the result of my ignorance about much of the newest research being done.

Edward Isham made two demands on me: to tell and to make sense of his story. The former task required the latter, especially if the complexities of Isham's seemingly straightforward and brutal life were to be recognized. No historian provided richer possibilities for interpreting Isham than Bertram Wyatt-Brown, whose landmark *Southern Honor* emphasizes how the "ancient ethic" of honor "was the cement that held regional culture together."[8] Although in some ways Isham stood outside of Wyatt-Brown's conception of honor—Isham's "shamelessness," after all, pitted his sense of reputation against the "respectability" of the community that tried him for murder—Wyatt-Brown provided an overarching, interpretive framework within which one individual could be situated.[9] Bereft of both economic security and stable personal relationships, Isham nevertheless possessed a sense of personal honor which demanded that no challenge to his physical prowess, his possession of a woman, or his meager claim to economic survival could go unaddressed. At the same time, he lived far enough outside the more widely accepted code of honor defining social relationships in the Sherrills Ford community that no one who insulted him, especially a farmer of substance who had denied him a wage decreed fair by a magistrate, was safe from his ferocity.

As important as this framework was (the modern historian's findings are too closely tied to specific contexts to lay claim to theory) it paled before two fundamental aspects of Wyatt-Brown's narrative. The first appeared simple enough, but it offered an encouraging rationale for my approach to Isham. "The scholar is dependent upon written records," Wyatt-Brown wrote of the limitations that the historian must acknowledge, "whereas feelings and even the dramas of daily routine often were conveyed by gesture, look, or silence, or words that no one saw fit to write down. We do, however, have an underutilized body of materials—courtroom testimony hidden away in county seats and state repositories."[10] Isham's words would have escaped us if not for the fragments contained in court testimony and, of course, the autobiography Schenck preserved in his notebook, presumably recorded as a lawyer's preparation for defending a hopeless case. In addition, newspaper advertisements for Isham's arrest contain recollections of his physical appearance, mannerisms, and behavior.[11] The kind of documentary evidence that Wyatt-Brown described as "indispensable" to his work had fallen into my lap.[12] To be sure, Isham's story defied broader quantitative analysis. The uniqueness of the sources documenting his life may preclude a detailed comparison with other poor whites living in the antebellum South, and his behavior was certainly too outrageous to be fairly interpreted as typical of his social class, but his story's narrative power allowed significant questions about violence, transience, economic survival, and societal tensions to be asked, even if they could not be answered definitively.

"Storytelling is the oldest form of history," Wyatt-Brown wrote in *Southern Honor*, satisfying "a basic human curiosity to learn how it all came out."[13] Of course, the historian seeks to do more than show how the story came out—arriving at "an understanding of social structure and the changes and tensions that constantly undermine the walls until they crumble and new ones take their place" is crucial.[14] Wyatt-Brown suggests that these two reasons, ancient and modern, for telling stories are separate from each other, whereas in truth stories explain the world they inhabit as well as satisfy curiosity about endings. Nevertheless, Wyatt-Brown's persuasive utilization of narrative testified to the hold a story can exert on the historian's imagination.

Still, the question lingered as to how much could be made of an anonymous life. Carl Bridenbaugh, in "Violence and Virtue in Virginia, 1766; or, The Importance of the Trivial," had shown how the seeming triviality of a colonial murder case, when "examined in connection with other contemporary events of historical importance . . . assumes an unrecognized significance."[15] The crime of Colonel John Chiswell, who killed the drunken merchant Robert Routledge in a tavern at Cumberland Court House, assumes a significance beyond the sensationalism of the event, especially as it occurred at a time when nascent public opinion in Virginia was increasingly critical of an aristocratic ruling class besieged by the Stamp Act crisis. "This unfortunate incident furnishes posterity with a richly detailed case history revealing just exactly how an aristocracy acts when it is in danger or merely threatened. Among themselves aristocrats will be democratic, . . . but they always present a solid, silent phalanx to the rest of society whether their cause be just or unjust, good or bad, right or wrong."[16] Routledge, however, had a following of those who wanted to see Chiswell prosecuted, and Chiswell was an influential man whose aristocratic friends resisted seeing one of their own brought before the bar. The murder, at least at the time, was hardly an obscure one. Did Isham's less-debated crime similarly reveal barely concealed tensions in antebellum culture?

The realization that a murder could reveal a societal fault line offered a way of understanding what happened when the transient laborer Edward Isham knifed the slaveholding farmer James

Cornelius. This killing in particular threatened an established social order, with frightening consequences, especially since it was conducted in the presence of slaves (none of whom, of course, could testify in court to what they had seen). Isham's subsequent capture was aided by the offer of a substantial reward and the printing of handbills, some of which reached Tennessee by stagecoach just as Isham arrived there. It appeared that little expense would be spared to secure the murderer's arrest.

Cornelius was not the first victim to die at Isham's hand. In fact, Isham had assumed his alias, Hardaway Bone, when he fled Alabama, where he had fired a shotgun into the chest of a man with whom he had had a running feud. Jim Runnels, the victim, however, was of Isham's social class. Although Isham had found it necessary to flee Alabama, he showed no concern that he might be tracked down over such a distance. The evidence is thin, but it suggests that greater resources were brought to bear after Cornelius' murder than after Runnels'. Isham's outrageous behavior knew no bounds, but when his actions crossed an important social class line, he was more than just chased out of state; he was arrested, prosecuted, and punished. The murder assumed a greater significance because it dramatized the plight of being poor and white in the antebellum South.

Other historians were also turning their attention to the obscure and finding greater significance. In *Celia, A Slave*, Melton A. McLaurin premised his research on the argument "that the personal and the political are never separate entities."[17] McLaurin recounted the 1855 killing by a Missouri slave named Celia of her sexually abusive master, John Newsom. Despite Celia's gruesome disposal of Newsom's body by burning it in the fireplace of her cabin, her crime was quickly discovered and she was brought to trial. The killing of a prominent and respected farmer by one of his slaves would seem to present little difficulty to her prosecution. However, her chief lawyer, John Jameson, realized nothing was easy in an atmosphere increasingly charged with the moral debate over slavery that was generated by the Kansas–Nebraska Act. If slaves were not supposed to kill their masters, neither were their masters—operating within a supposedly benevolent institution—supposed to rape their slaves. Celia's case provided incontrovertible evidence that both things had happened, and the moral implications raised by incidents such as this one discomforted a slaveholding society increasingly called upon to defend its practice.

McLaurin believed that "the lives of lesser figures, men and women who lived and died in virtual anonymity, often better illustrate certain aspects of the major issues than do the lives of those who, through significant achievement, the appeal of the orator, or the skill of the polemicist, achieve national prominence."[18] This argument helped me look anew at Isham and ponder the exact circumstances of his crime. Rarely, if ever, had Isham interacted in meaningful ways with prominent citizens; not surprisingly, his circle of acquaintances tended to be from similar backgrounds. At the same time, there seemed to be an easy familiarity between Isham and Cornelius.

On the Sunday morning of his death, as he washed for church, James Cornelius spotted Isham approaching his house, whereupon he invited him (according to Isham) to come in. Austin Cornelius later testified at Isham's trial that his dying brother had told him he felt no fear of Isham. Even so, James was standing in the presence of a notoriously short-tempered man he had refused to pay for digging ditches on his farm, even going so far as staying a magistrate's decision that had awarded Isham most of what he had asked for (the result of what must have been the only legal action in which Isham willingly participated!). What kind of unspoken social relationship existed between the two men that allowed the prosperous farmer to hail the common laborer, or enabled the cheated worker to directly confront the niggardly landowner? If, as historians have argued in recent years, antebellum society was rife with class resentment which the travails of the Civil War exacerbated,[19] then perhaps Isham can also be seen as someone whose life of "exploitation, hardships and repression," in E. P. Thompson's words, "continually exposes the text of paternalist theatre to ironic criticism and (less frequently) to revolt."[20] There is good reason to balance a view of Isham as acting out of his own, idiosyncratic rage with one that also asks what it meant to be a poor white struggling for economic survival in the antebellum South.

Historians, then, were providing examples of how isolated actions might possess important hidden meanings. And, to my delight, I was discovering how fashionable it had become for them to admit to storytelling. John Demos, for example, says in *The Unredeemed Captive*—his account of the 1704 adoption of a Puritan minister's captive daughter by a Mohawk family who lived at a Jesuit mission-fort near Montreal—"Most of all, I wanted to write a *story*" (author's emphasis).[21] By contrast, Simon Schama, in *Landscape and Memory*, sought to extend the sense of childhood wonder he experienced from reading Rudyard Kipling's story *Puck of Pook's Corner*—filled with visions of the peoples who across the ages had stood on the same spot of land—to a belief that landscape's scenery "is built up as much from strata of memory as from layers of rock."[22] Both historians depended on narrative to recover memories nearly lost, yet both also wanted to tie their work to the modern world. For Demos, the connection came by recognizing how his tale of seventeenth-century captivity resonated with our experiences of Tehran, Lebanon, various "hijackings," and Patty Hearst. Like the experience of the abducted Eunice Williams and her family, our "contact across the lines of race and culture remains a lively, often painful, theme in our modern 'global village.'"[23] The attitude taken by Schama is, if anything, more direct, as he expresses the hope that his journey "may help us keep faith with a future on this tough, lovely old planet."[24]

Storytelling, then, is rarely an idle undertaking, and, as my research grew, I returned to a question that had lingered from my first encounter with Edward Isham: Why was this man, apparently possessing few redeeming qualities, so compelling an individual that I wanted to tell his story? Isham was many things: a fighter and golddigger in Georgia, a gambler in Tennessee, a cattle-driver in Alabama, a rail-splitter in Arkansas, and a farmer in North Carolina, but never was he so garish and cartoonish a figure as Jeeter Lester, the poor white cropper of *Tobacco Road*. Isham somehow maintained an identity which, if it did not make him a sympathetic figure, at least prompted consideration of what lay behind his viciousness.

The evidence that best persuades me of Isham's humanity came from late in my research, although it neatly epitomizes his life's turmoil. In his autobiography, Isham tells of a wife he took in North Carolina. Schenck recorded her name as Mandy Lesley, daughter of James Lesley; she is probably the Amanda Lasley listed in the 1850 federal census report for Iredell County.[25] Mandy became pregnant by Isham—by then called Hardaway Bone—but she died at the time their child was born. Aside from commenting that his child was staying at the home of the Reed family, Isham said nothing more about the infant, omitting even a reference to gender.

The child—a daughter, as other sources revealed—outlived her father by many years. William and Susan Reed had no choice but to keep this child born of a mother who never knew her and a father who was hanged. In the 1860 federal census, taken in Catawba County a few weeks after Isham's execution, the Reed family counted six children in their household, including the one-year-old girl named Margaret Bone.[26] Ten years later, with the next federal census, the family had moved to neighboring Iredell County; Margaret was still living with William and Susannah Reid (the family name spelled differently), while their son James Reid and his family lived in the adjoining household.[27]

It is the report of the 1880 federal census, however, that most pointedly records Edward Isham's legacy. At this time, Margaret Boone, as she was then listed, appeared as a young woman aged twenty-two and living in the household of thirty-three-year-old James Reid (neither William nor Susan appeared in the report).[28] Two questions were asked in this census which were not incorporated into earlier ones. The first asked where each household member's father had been born. The second asked for the relationship between the listed individual and the head of the household. The responses show that Margaret's father had been born in Georgia and that she was a boarder in the Reid household.

Perhaps too much can be read into these laconic statements of fact, but they are inescapably poignant. Margaret Bone, carrying Isham's alias throughout her life, knew of her father's birthplace; did she not also know, therefore, of his restless life and ignoble death? She would have known no parents other than the Reeds, and, yet, twenty years after she came into their home, having grown up with their children, she was described as a boarder. Edward Isham appeared to be at ease only in the rough-and-tumble region of the Georgia frontier, although, even there, he was constantly at odds with someone. Always the outsider, the loner, the unwanted visitor, Isham inadvertently seemed to pass along his most notable characteristic to his daughter. Was she, too, the outsider, an individual who could never escape the memories other people had of the bad man she had not known?

I have known this child, as I realize that I have known something of her father. Part of Isham's strangeness to a modern audience results from our inability to understand what it is like to live so marginalized an existence. To historians and teachers alike, sharing as they do middle-class ties, the combination of Isham's behavior, which raises images of stereotypical poor white behavior; and the fact that his life is carefully recorded in his own voice, a preoccupation usually of the middle class, strikes us as incongruous, even unsettling. As a teacher, however, I heard his voice echo in familiar ways in the voices of many of the children who have sat in my classroom.

Although I am not aware of a student ever having threatened me, and I have not personally witnessed the kind of destructiveness Isham wrought, I have been in the presence of children I suspected were never heard. They may have yelled with their lives, living in apparent defiance of everyone around them; or they may have lived in sullen silence, but they were regarded both by parents and society at large as unneeded and unwanted. Some of them responded remarkably, even pathetically, to whatever extra attention I could offer as a teacher, while others seemed too far away in their thoughts for me to reach. Their behavior was the result of indifference or misplaced attention that focused more on the needs of their parents. I felt as if I had seen something of their lives in the life of Edward Isham. Over and again I wondered what chance Isham had in life when, as a child, he came home from school crying to his father that he had been beaten by a boy who held him by his hair, only to have his father respond by cutting off his locks so that he might be more likely to whip his opponent. If anything, Margaret Bone may have had an even less of a chance, with her mother dead, her father repeatedly drunk in the few months he was with her, and growing up knowing him only through the ugly account she was told.

This is not simply the harrowing account of a father's dissolution; nor is it a maudlin story about a little match girl who, in this instance, failed to see her angelic mother in the dying glow of a struck match. Behind the scream of rage that was his life is Isham's voice, as level as the detached voice in his autobiography. The man who constantly "got into a difficulty," as he euphemistically described his fights, was an individual for whom life itself was a difficulty.[29] With his gold mining, his lumber cutting, his cattle driving, his gambling, his beekeeping, his farming, he indirectly asks us how well we could survive in a world whose economy insured our marginality. Inured to a life in which the best fighter was the best man, Isham causes us to reflect on how we define honor. Having turned to the court for a redress of his grievances only to find that influence had blocked his way, Isham makes us ponder the certainty of justice.

All this does not mean that Edward Isham was simply the unwitting victim of forces he could not control. He is not, after all, representative of the quiet and truly anonymous, if at times equally desperate, lives of poor whites in the antebellum South. Isham's poverty and transience were reinforced by his tendency toward violence, a personal characteristic so constantly exhibited that it marked him even in a region noted for the fierceness of its people. Only when we embrace a sense of contingency—that is, a belief in "historical events as a series of real choices that living people actually made," as David Hackett Fischer has defined it—can narrative have the power to move us with its uncertainty.[30] Isham may have careened across the South during his brief life, but the incident that brought him to the gallows was not inevitable. It was contingent upon a string of coincident events—a wife's death, the loss of a crop, a decline into unrelieved drunkenness, and the staying of a magistrate's order—that prompted a calculated decision to assault Cornelius.

For me, the narrative tension of Isham's life was palpable because I have seen how adolescence often represents for young people a last opportunity—perhaps increasingly tenuous given our hyperkinetic pushing children into the stresses and vices that afflict us—to secure an identity with which they can comfortably live. With too many students, I was never sure what identity had formed inside the outward defensive gestures that protect us from one another; this may not have mattered in studying the past, but I could not separate what I taught from who the learners were. Similarly, I was able to read Isham's account and wonder what kind of individual lay behind his frightful persona. For this reason alone, Edward Isham, the poor white laborer, deserved the attention that his contemporaries more readily afforded Hardaway Bone, the convicted killer.

Ultimately, my understanding of Isham depended on understanding myself as a teacher. Storytelling should come easily for teachers, even those in high school who fear that adolescents will resist what appears to be too childish. If historians in recent years have felt the pull toward narrative as a way to escape the abstractness, false certainty, and relentless inevitability imposed by numbers, then I felt a need to show—perhaps to myself, most of all—that as a teacher I also fashion narrative to create a sense of the past.

The difference between the roles of historian and teacher, unfortunately, is the difference between the creation of knowledge and the transmission of culture. However, what most immediately concerned me was not the resulting hierarchy these differing roles might signify, or even why teaching has been so enervated of playful creativity, but how the roles might be combined.

What seemed important for me at first was to capitalize on a historical find by publishing a formal historical treatise. Only when I was well along in this work did I realize the depths of dissatisfaction I felt as a public school history teacher. Henry Giroux has described the importance of teachers acting as "transformative intellectuals"—that is, actively assuming "responsibility for raising serious questions about what they teach, how they are to teach, and what the larger goals are for which they are striving."[31] With Edward Isham, I was engaged in work that was both enjoyable and meaningful, and yet which did not appear to fit easily into my classroom responsibilities. Isham (or anything I could relate to him) did not fit into any of the curriculum objectives; nor would he be of help with final examinations. The realization that, as a teacher, I had surprisingly little role in deciding what I did in my classroom was becoming apparent.

Teachers rarely are expected to address fundamental issues in education. The educational psychologist speaks to issues of child development, the administrator defines how public concerns are addressed and the bureaucrat determines course content. Classroom teachers are left to devise gaming strategies for implementing the curriculum objectives they have been handed, which is perceived to be safe enough work for the women, coaches, and local history buffs who fill public school history departments (not to denigrate these individuals, who have the stamina—or, occasionally, dullness—to survive the relentless din of boosting test score achievement and preparing students for the job market). Considering the part-time, primarily female world out of which public schools grew, and the assembly-line, factory worker world in which they received their modern cast, it is not surprising that the teacher's experience has been largely ignored. At the same time, if "woman/worker" teachers are left with little responsibility for deciding how their subject should be presented, the reason for their disempowerment may also have much to do with how history is perceived.

As understood in the public school setting, culture has been—using Michael Apple's description—"commodified," instead of being taught on the continuous struggle embodied in lived experience.[32] Heaven knows public education, already the battleground for conflicting interests about what is good for society, has ample reason for refusing to define education as anything more than providing background information or communication skills. Because we define ourselves through our past, history provides a supreme arena for controversy over how to transmit a cultural understanding of who we, a diverse people, are. We pretend, however, that we can talk of the past as if it were a lifeless object detached from ourselves. When the past is ordered by carefully demarcated historical eras with a nod given to every major topic, there is little chance for realizing what Walter Benjamin has asserted is the present's "unique experience with the past."[33] All our todays (and the facts with which they are crammed) meld with our yesterdays, stretching eternally into the past, except that our todays are better days, and are then appended in updated chapters at the end of the book. We fail to ask how the uniqueness of our times might direct our inquiries into times past; instead, we rely on the mere chronicling of events. No wonder students accuse history of being boring. Sensing how we neuter the past by presenting it as an uninterrupted stream leading to the present, they respond to it in the same manner with which they treat a grandparent's homily about the old days, with occasional amusement at the quaint tales and frequent contempt when called to be thankful. Do we hesitate to converse with the past because we agree with Walter Benjamin that the past's claim upon us cannot be settled cheaply?[34]

Public education surely must be afraid to confront any historical problem that eludes an answer or elicits paradox or encourages debate. That identity is not fixed but must be refined in the heat of our controversy with the past is a suggestion that is at odds with a public school system predicated upon arriving at consensus. History as taught in public schools, like advertising, offers us problems that are effortlessly resolved by the proper dosage of the democratic spirit. Squeezed out of this formula is the sense that the past itself is rife with tension and, moreover, exists in tension with the present. How can we tell a tale of antebellum poverty and violence without thinking of—indeed, without our story being influenced by—our present culture's poverty and violence? To forego exploring the ways in which we understand the past as we write its history means that our stories are less honest, less probing, less forthrightly revealing of ourselves—as well as our predecessors—than they might be. Our lived experiences require us to converse with, not simply address or listen to, the past with which we are tied.

Part of my motivation in this undertaking, therefore, sprang from the desire to demonstrate my belief that the teacher as historian could bring skills and insights to the public school classroom that would aid students in thinking of knowledge and their learning as organic, not static. How, for example, does the documentation of Isham's life challenge what we think we know about the past? From this point, we can begin to ask specific questions about Isham—his labor, his relations with women or black southerners, for example—that would guide our study. The creative process of engaging a historical personage is important, not for fostering an appreciation of antebellum history, but because it reveals how we choose what we say of the past, the source of our truths about who we are.

"[T]he truths that mean most to us must always be uttered by halves," warns a nobleman to the young protagonist in Umberto Eco's seventeenth-century setting of *The Island of the Day Before.*[35] Such worldly caution turns to more deadly evil, however, when we pretend our half-truths possess certainty about a past we can never know with completeness. Perhaps more than access to the information revolution, students need to understand how knowledge, embedded with our values, is always in flux, representing as it does our restless creativity. My grand hope was that the example of one teacher bringing his imagination to one small historical problem might cause a student to see learning as a liberator of his or her own creative energies.

Also involved in this undertaking was my sympathy for the voice of someone who had been ignored both in his lifetime and for years afterward. Isham represented a fleeting image of the past that threatened "to disappear irretrievably" if "not recognized by the present as one of its own concerns."[36] There is a difference between observing that Isham was an obscure individual in his day and believing that he deserves this status in our own. The difference lies in the consideration that Isham speaks to concerns we hold that his contemporaries did not. Not only does he tell us something of a poor white's experience in the antebellum South, his story strikes sympathetic tones in an era when poverty, violence, and transience are increasingly evident and bear the tensions between social classes and racial groupings. Isham's life allows the historian "to brush history against the grain," in Benjamin's striking phrase, because it observes that the "anonymous toil" of laborers, not to mention enslaved people, was required to support a civilization, the artifacts and accomplishments of which have received the greater attention.[37]

My research drew on the work of historians who have recognized the web of social, economic, and political relations that defined life in the antebellum South. The history I taught in the classroom, however, so emphasized a chain of being in which causes and events comprised the links that there was no place for asking how and why the chain had been fashioned in the first place. I understood, of course, how this approach fit with the history of a nation described as "triumphant," in which hegemony was as unchallengeable as the answers to the course's multiple choice tests. However, this view of history did not square with what I found in school, at least in the classes filled with the children of hosiery and furniture workers, where students took little interest in a subject that appeared so remote from their existence. Unable to find meaning for their lives in the stories they were told, the students concluded that history was yet another instrument of control over them, a conclusion that had also become increasingly difficult for me to escape.

What I had not encountered in my teaching experience was someone who could describe my students' lives as simply and clearly, if chillingly, as Isham. Did he have anything to say that might make a life of economic insignificance and personal alienation easier to understand? Could what I had experienced as a teacher help render Isham in human colors that were warmer than the cold facts of his crime? Were Isham's story brought to my students, perhaps they might see that not only could they create history, but that they *were* the stuff of history.

Students were the stuff of history in one fundamental way: their lives were commentary on the past. In a culture that prides itself on embodying beliefs in equality and opportunity, the lived experiences of students testified to the degree those promises went unfulfilled. Excluded from even the imperfect examples of the social construction called history does not disallow students from arguing with the past. To cast themselves as hopeless "products" of a deterministic history required surrendering the part of their humanity that insists upon choice. While many students may never feel a connection with the famous and powerful in their textbooks, they can, nevertheless, ask questions about them. Once they begin to exhibit "courage, humor, cunning, and fortitude" in asking why their lives are ordered the way they are, students "will constantly call in question every victory, past and present, of the rulers."[38] They may, on occasion, find that the answers are more complex than wooden exploitative or cynical conspiratorial theories might suggest, but the "critical apprehension of our real existing lives" can steer them away from the "empty moralism" and "sterile scienticism" that plague public education.[39]

But deeper by far than these factors and, finally, what moved me most, was a desire to secure an identity for myself that would confirm a wavering belief that I could engage in significant, creative work, even as I had to accept the grim realities of employment in a public school. I needed to affirm a belief that my work was important in the intellectual ways that mattered to me; and that I was not simply too late or too lazy or too unfortunate to be a member of academia, where "real" intellectual work takes place. Public schools, embodying so much of our culture's ambivalence toward both learning and children, are not likely places to find such assurance; neither are universities, which often seem to view the public schools as wards from which the lucky few will escape to find enlightenment on their campuses.

Faith in the creative intelligence of young people, and in my own, however, required a tangible demonstration if it was to remain honest. All points in the past are equidistant from our culture's interests in freedom, equality, opportunity, security, community, and individuality in that each can show us how these issues have been understood (which is not to deny that some eras place these issues in greater relief). Despite his obscurity, Edward Isham's short, frenzied existence had something to say about these issues. Significance and obscurity, in fact, are not antonymous; the former represents a value judgment made by the present on the past. Learning to make those judgments for oneself is perhaps the most difficult lesson in one's education. Apart from all the curricula guides, this is still of primary importance to the public school teacher, who remains the great generalist in education and hopes that lessons in making judgment have broader applicability in evaluating society.

A student in a public school may never be asked to consider whether or not something has significance. Students must rely, instead, on what they are told on the authority of others, whether they be teachers, textbook authors, or designers of the course of study. Young people already ask about the relevance of their studies, that is, if they have not been so panicked by their economic prospects as to accept whatever they are told must be done if they are to succeed. What they lack, and what a society adrift needs so desperately, are teachers who can lead them in examining their lives in the context of their culture in order to explore the interaction between the two. Both individual and culture are the descendants of countless choices made, willingly or unwillingly, knowingly and unknowingly. The history of one individual, and how that history was created, can serve as a beginning point for an extended dialogue about who we are.

Teachers, unfortunately, are so harried by the increasing demands both of students who have been discarded by others and a system of education struggling to retain public support that they must struggle to raise serious questions about what they do. Indeed, were public education fearful of inquiring teachers, it could scarcely better insure that such queries were not raised. The closed system that is public education, in which teaching, learning, and testing form a self-referencing circle of schooling, is well insulated from questions about how we know what is important. As these questions often elude definitive answers, asking them assumes greater importance, yet it is this tentativeness and a willingness to admit the limits of our knowledge that public education finds so hard to accept.

Ultimately, a teacher who seriously pursues questions of purpose and meaning finds inspiration outside of education's professional circles. Abraham Joshua Heschel taught that the Sabbath makes *time*, or history, sacred, not *space*, or place. The Sabbath, therefore, helps us displace the coveting of things in space with the coveting of things in time.[40] The historian reaches across time to find someone who both resembles and differs from ourselves. Coveting this knowledge may bring miraculous creations in which we feel almost at one with the past, so intimately do we feel its closeness. As with the sacred, however, we can never fully know the past, and so our sense of accomplishment is tinged with wistfulness.

We feel that we know the profane Edward Isham not simply because we have so many details of his life, but because we can recognize his life in our own. Compassion lies at the heart of teaching. Without it, the teacher dispenses with the one attribute most needed for an individual to reach out to another in the hope that learning will enrich living. When brought to the historian's work, compassion helps forestall the treating of a historical personage as a "subject," as evidence of the scientism that reduces people to objects and elevates the inquirer to omniscience.

Left unresolved, and perhaps incapable of being resolved, is the question of whether a story like Isham's tells us more about the historical period being studied or the one in which the story is being addressed. My suspicion is that historians would emphasize the importance of the former while taking the risk of not adequately exploring the significance of the latter. I know that Isham's story would have been told differently, assuming that it was told at all, if other attitudes, experiences, and talents had been brought to bear. In such ways we become a part of the stories we tell, and they part of us. Remembering our tangled, sometimes unspoken, and even unrecognized connections with our stories saves us from the hubris of thinking we can know all.

Notes

[1] The statements in this paragraph regarding Edward Isham are more fully elaborated in Scott P. Culclasure, "'I Have Killed a Damned Dog': Murder by a Poor White in the Antebellum South," *North Carolina Historical Review* LXX (January 1993): 14–39 and reprinted in Bolton and Culclasure, *The Confessions of Edward Isham.*

[2] Joyce Appleby, Lynn Hunt, and Margaret Jacob, *Telling the Truth about History* (New York: W. W. Norton & Company, 1994) 88–9, 148–51.

[3] William Faulkner, *Absalom, Absalom!* in *Novels, 1936–1940* (New York: Library of America, 1990) 18.

[4] Appleby et al. 233.

[5] David Schenck, *A Memorial Volume of the Guilford Battle Ground Company* (Greensboro, N. C.: Charles L. Van Noppen, 1893). Schenck's best-known history, zealously defending North Carolina's contributions to the Revolution, is *North Carolina, 1780–'81; Being a History of the Invasion of the Carolinas by the British* (Raleigh, N. C.: Edwards & Broughton, 1889).

[6] David Schenck Notebook, "Biography of Edward Icem alias 'Hardaway Bone,'" 23–49, David Schenck Papers, Private Papers, State Archives, Division of Archives and History, Raleigh.

[7] Schenck's sentiments about these themes are freely and repeatedly expressed in the nineteen volumes of his diaries kept throughout most of his life. See the David Schenck Books, Southern Historical Collection, University of North Carolina Library, Chapel Hill.

[8] Bertram Wyatt-Brown, *Southern Honor: Ethics and Behavior in the Old South* (New York: Oxford University Press, 1982) xv.

[9] On shamelessness, see Wyatt-Brown 59, 398–9, 402.

[10] Wyatt-Brown xi.

[11] For an example of one newspaper advertisement, see Culclasure, "'I Have Killed a Damned Dog'" 31 and also Appendix C in Bolton and Culclasure, *The Confessions of Edward Isham.*

[12] Wyatt-Brown xi.

[13] Wyatt-Brown xiv.

[14] Wyatt-Brown xiv.

[15] Carl Bridenbaugh, "Violence and Virtue in Virginia, 1766; or, The Importance of the Trivial" in *Early Americans,* ed. Carl Bridenbaugh (New York: Oxford University Press, 1981) 211.

[16] Bridenbaugh 211.

[17] Melton A. McLaurin, *Celia, A Slave* (Athens, Georgia: University of Georgia Press, 1991) xi.

[18] McLaurin xi.

[19] For a recent treatment of the theme of class resentment, see Charles C. Bolton, *Poor Whites of the Antebellum South: Tenants and Laborers in Central North Carolina and Northeast Mississippi* (Durham, N. C.: Duke University Press, 1994).

[20] Thompson 11.

[21] John Demos, *The Unredeemed Captive: A Family Story from Early America* (New York: Alfred A. Knopf, 1994) xi.

[22] Simon Schama, *Landscape and Memory* (New York: Alfred A. Knopf, 1995) 7.

[23] Demos xii.

[24] Schama 19.

[25] Seventh Census of the United States, 1850: Iredell County, North Carolina, Population Schedule.

[26] Eighth Census of the United States, 1860: Catawba County, North Carolina, Population Schedule.

[27] Ninth Census of the United States, 1870: Iredell County, North Carolina, Population Schedule.

[28] Tenth Census of the United States, 1880: Iredell County, North Carolina, Population Schedule.

[29] For example, "I got into a difficulty with a negro about a fishing pole and tried to cut him but was prevented, for this they turned me out of the church." Schenck Notebook 24.

[30] David Hackett Fischer, *Paul Revere's Ride* (New York: Oxford University Press, 1994) xv and note 4, 375.

[31] Henry A. Giroux, *Teachers As Intellectuals: Toward a Critical Pedagogy of Learning* (South Hadley, Massachusetts: Bergin and Garvey, 1990) 126.

[32] Michael W. Apple, *Education and Power* (New York: Routledge and Kegan Paul, 1983) 74.

[33] Walter Benjamin, "Theses on the Philosophy of History," in *Illuminations*, ed. Hannah Arendt (New York: Schocken Books, 1969) 262.

[34] Benjamin 254.

[35] Umberto Eco, *The Island of the Day Before* (New York: Harcourt Brace & Company, 1995) 112.

[36] Benjamin 255.

[37] Benjamin 256-7.

[38] Benjamin 254.

[39] Svi Shapiro, *Between Capitalism and Democracy: Educational Policy and the Crisis of the Welfare State* (South Hadley, Massachusetts: Bergin and Garvey, 1990) 27.

[40] Abraham Joshua Heschel, *The Sabbath: Its Meaning for Modern Man* (New

York: Farrar, Straus and Giroux, 1951) 90–1.

Chapter 3

Teacher as Apostle of Dangerous Memory

Despite the amount of information lost to us, staggering heaps of documents from the nineteenth century still exist and can be found in the most ordinary places. Consider, for example, a scrap of paper, found at a flea market, that once was part of the store accounts kept by Henry M. Mills of Granite Hill in Iredell County, North Carolina, bearing this scrawled message: "Marche 14 57 lete cela hav too pears of scus. . . ." The note was signed by R. K. Henry, and Mills added to the bottom, "I sent 1 pr. shoes $1.50 March 14th 1857." In the context of similar messages found in the same cardboard box, one can surmise that this request for shoes was carried from the farmer to the storekeeper by a slave: Adam A. McNeely asked Mills that his "boy Sam" be allowed a hat charged to his account; T. P. Gillespie requested that "too dollars" on his account be given to the "boy Garrison"; and Theos. Allison desired that "if they is iney letter in the office" it be sent by the unnamed boy, adding that "if that big jar aint gon to day lay it away for me till I come down."[1]

Notes like these lend a human touch to an inhumane institution. Unlike in census reports, the slaves mentioned in the notes often are referred to by name; the everyday needs of sometimes barely literate masters are communicated, the function of a storekeeper is illustrated. True, life's essence is gone from the notes. Was the "boy Sam" really a child, and was Garrison sent because he was trustworthy and liked by his master, and did any of these individuals—slave, master, or storekeeper—reflect on their relationships with each other? In spite of what they do not tell us, however, these scraps of information encourage inquiry into how a community distributed power to create a way of life. Most of all, they remind us what is easy to forget in an era more attuned to totalitarian politics: The practice of slavery involved people who knew each other, sometimes intimately, and who lived with each other in a complex web of relationships that, while incomprehensible to us in some ways, nevertheless involved familiar issues of power.

While it would perhaps be unfair to expect such a small scale to be the sole one used in history textbooks, the impersonal way in which most public school texts treat the issue of slavery—so central to an understanding of our past—is tortuous. It is not that textbooks ignore the institution, but what they emphasize is the political controversy generated by its practice. The everyday world inhabited by slaves, masters, and merchants is shunted in favor of a political realm dominated by the famous and influential. Because of the caution with which textbooks are written—they must be adopted, after all, by political agencies that are hypersensitive to public controversy—detailed descriptions of slavery are avoided, apparently on the assumption that discussion of past wrongs promotes present divisions. Instead of stories about power and survival, hope and anguish, relationship and community, we are left with encyclopedic entries devoid of human passion. Even the most sophisticated textbooks rarely go beyond issues of historiography—what the famous and influential intellectuals have said about the subject—to teach students how they might approach a past world which continues to influence the culture in which they live. Connections between past and present are left ambiguous, and societal relationships are defined only in terms of the formal institutions that rest upon unseen arrangements of power.

For example, in *American Voices*, a respectable textbook commonly found in public high schools, four paragraphs are devoted to describing how slavery worked, matched by the same number of paragraphs outlining life in the industrial North. These paragraphs are followed by three entire sections composed of many paragraphs that trace the political treatment of slavery in the period between the Mexican War and the election of 1860.[2] To be sure, what is said in the four paragraphs reflects sound scholarship and a compassionate tone: "Treatment of slaves varied widely—from paternal and benign to incredibly cruel—but in all cases slaves were considered to be pieces of property, not people."[3] Nevertheless, the presence of common people is noticeably absent; the illustrations and the one supplemental reading at the end of the chapter that features a former slave's memory of her mother only partially overcome the anonymity with which the text treats the topic.[4] The authors may have succeeded in avoiding a detailed description of slavery's more painful aspects, but they have also failed to help students understand how thoroughly this arrangement of social, economic, and political relationships defined everyday life in this era. Vibrant historical communities that students might compare with the ones in which they live do not exist.

Absent most tellingly is an open-ended consideration of how a culture that feverishly enshrined the tenants of the Declaration of Independence could simultaneously and unblushingly claim the right to own human beings. The point in asking this question is not to condemn the culture, for few enterprises are more foolish than upbraiding the dead for failing to share the righteousness of the living. In fact, the point is to do exactly what most textbooks and, by extension, the public schools that depend upon them, most fear: to ask of the present, with its unfulfilled promises, how it came to be. We recognize that the present cannot answer without reference to the past, hence the purpose of history. When we call upon the past as a witness to its experiences, we may be surprised by the clarity of its speech, as T. S. Eliot understood (in what might be an epitaph for Edward Isham):

> And what the dead had no speech for, when living,
> They can tell you, being dead: the communication
> Of the dead is tongued with fire beyond the language of the living.[5]

What Eliot explicitly understood, and what the textbook implicitly recognizes, is that the communication of the dead is dangerous because it challenges our presuppositions of a past too static, too detached, to have much relation to present-day circumstances. The dead will talk with tongues of fire when we understand that they are talking to us, not to each other, with voices that tell of the promise, fulfillment, and disappointment they once knew; voices that their contemporaries may have ignored but which speak to us of the injustice and oppression that have tragically accompanied our nation's promise of freedom and opportunity.

Behind the textbook's political caution lies a subtler, more insidious message about the relationship between student, text, and subject. Despite its superior scholarship in a variety of historical fields (and its lofty title is ably underwritten by several important American historians), this textbook emphasizes a political history for students. There is an irony in the political safeness of relating a political history. Past political controversies, no matter how divisive and significant, usually appear remote to the everyday world of people who live in the present and without much access to power. A textbook might more comfortably relate the deeds of a great statesman, or the debate surrounding a piece of legislation, or the rise of a new political party—examples that can neatly be objectified for the purposes of measuring student "achievement"—than the social constructions that allocated, in ways that were often resistant to change, freedom, justice, and opportunity. Instead, political histories tend to concentrate on the people who were used to dealing with power in controversies that are given clearly defined beginnings and endings. Of course, the past's reality was different, with political leaders working in a world that was replete with human uncertainty, inconsistency, and contingency. The tentativeness of much of what they did and the less easily discernible web of relationships out of which they operated, however, escape the textbook's narrative. Little room is left for ambiguity, much less paradox, because of the expectation of arriving at "lessons" that will make straight our present paths.

Textbooks only reflect our own hesitancy to raise questions about race, class, gender, work, faith, community, or any other concern that might challenge students to search out their rootedness in the past by asking how these matters have been understood both yesterday and today. Instead of challenging students to do this, we expect them to be concerned with individuals whose lives seem as removed from their own as frock coats and hoop shirts are from blue jeans and birkenstocks or—perhaps more to the point—from the political leaders of our own time. While not denigrating the importance of either a chronology of events or historians' differing interpretations of their significance, our histories must also allow for the past's transcendent claim upon the present to be felt. The stories upon which we concentrate should be like our lives in the degree of complexity and uncertainty they exhibit. Most of all, they should educe questions of why relationships are defined as they are, questions that are important to ask if we are to decide whether to accept the past's legacy or to demand that the present be lived differently.

Textbooks, of course, are only one means to the end of encouraging students to root their identity in an understanding of the past. They cannot substitute for the personal interaction that occurs between teacher and student, as demonstrated by one unexpected moment when a lifetime of experience flashed by in an instant. The moment came at the end of the school year, a time which often evokes sentimentality from students. The comment one student made on a last day of class, however, left me pondering its meaning long afterward. Pausing as she was leaving the classroom, the student thanked me "for telling like it is." Her construction clearly used the present tense, even though she was referring to a history course (one in which students had examined the storekeeper's notes cited earlier). She was gone before I could ask her to explain, but since then I have wondered if she sensed something that I did not at the time. "What oppressed people understand better than most," observed Stanley Aronowitz and Henry Giroux, "is that intellectuals are typically servants of the mighty; they often provide the legitimacy for deeds of state, private violence, and exploitation."[6] Inasmuch as the teaching of history tends either to overwhelm with trivialities or to confirm the existing order—the former, in fact, may be a way of succeeding in the latter—the student had good reason for doubting the past's relevance to her life. In this class, however, we had talked of history with a view to identifying how it had shaped, for good or ill, the present. Our assumption was that understanding who we are, individually and collectively, depended upon a sense of rootedness in the past. The history we tried to tell (weakly, to be sure) depended more upon conversation with the past than revelation through it. The answers we arrived at, when we did, sometimes satisfied us and occasionally left us uncomfortable. Nevertheless, we sensed that looking into ourselves also required that we look outwardly to each other; none of our alienation was so great as to deny the relationships that bound us together in communities situated in time.

What was it we talked with the past about? Throughout *Four Quartets*, T. S. Eliot meditates upon the relationship between past and present:

> Footfalls echo in the memory
> Down the passage which we did not take
> Towards the door we never opened
> Into the rose-garden.[7]

To root an identity in the past means to ask after contingencies pursued and left unpursued, and to consider choices made or left unmade. Our purpose is not to enter a world of speculation about what might have been but to be conscious of how our moment in the present was shaped. Accepting a history text without expecting the past to be able to speak in alternative ways means accepting the present arrangements of power it offers as the only ones conceivable: political leaders truly in control, common people rendered as anonymous masses, complex communities reduced to terse paragraphs, all swept along by the steady and unbroken march of events. We are less in need of liberation from the past which brought us into being than from the histories which limit what we can know; histories that drown us with facts at the expense of meaning as related through narrative.

"Only through time time is conquered," Eliot wrote of how the past cannot be remembered except as we reference ourselves to it.[8] The histories related by others will assign us, if we allow them, an identity that separates us from the past that, in Walter Benjamin's memorable image, expected our coming.[9] As soon as we are disconnected from the past, we are left adrift in the present, susceptible to believing that the world is immutable. Walter Benjamin described the past as possessing "a *weak* Messianic power," hence the past's claim on us.[10] To study the past with the view of tracing the processes that frame our existence *delivers* us from the strictures of the present (hence the past's Messianic power, which is weak because we can choose to ignore it). Identities evolve over time, encompassing the experiences of a lifetime and the predispositions fostered by earlier identities, and cannot, therefore, be formulated for us by others. The past is alive with a cacophony of voices which will not be heard except when we assume the burden of soliciting them to speak.

Conjuring the past is risky, assuming that we want history to force an examination of how we live in the present. If we do, then we will seek out those stories in particular which challenge our assumptions about how life can, and should, be lived. Johann-Baptist Metz describes these stories as "dangerous memories," by which he refers to the

> memories that make demands on us. These are memories in which earlier experiences break through to the center point of our lives and reveal new and dangerous insights for the present. They illuminate for a few moments and with a harsh steady light the questionable nature of things we have apparently come to terms with, and show up the banality of our supposed "realism."[11]

There is in Metz's description a sense of the transitory moment, comparable to Benjamin's comment about the weakness of the past's Messianic power. These memories have not simply been forgotten; they have been subjected to the desire to be forever banished by power arrangements that find them inconveniently disquieting. Bringing them to people's attention is neither an easy nor a popular task, but as teachers we have little choice if we believe that education frees us to effect change in the world. We do not hold all these stories ourselves, nor can we tell them all, but we can engage our students to possess enough dangerous memory for them to decide how they want to live in the world.

The praxis for our liberation, however, does not come easily in a time when genuine self-identity, rooted in the past, is so difficult to create, as demonstrated with an illustration also drawn from experience in the classroom.[12] As he entered the classroom, the student handed me a worn, cheaply printed pamphlet with evident pride, for he had made a historical discovery unmentioned in the textbook. The pamphlet came from a relative of the student who had assured him that here was evidence of the white man's conspiracy to obfuscate historical truth. I had heard the pamphlet's story before, but I never had seen it in print, nor had I expected it to still be repeated so long after the life it described: Nearly three generations after his death, Warren G. Harding was being heralded as the first black President of the United States. The student had little notion of who Harding was, much less the origin of the story about Harding's ancestry which had been popularized by a bitter partisan, white supremacist, and economics professor named William Estabrook Chancellor who established something of a cottage industry by collecting wildly accusative and unsubstantiated gossip on the subject in the 1920s.[13] Myth was being celebrated as history by a young person who knew of injustice in the telling of only some stories but not how to make a personal, empowering connection with the past. So starved are we for a sense of who we are that we have concocted a toxic "memory-effect" (apologies to the postmodernists) that replaces honest struggle with what we can know of the past with the gullibility to believe whatever confirms our unexamined preconceptions.

The pathos behind this incident lies in how a discreditable, shopworn story originally told out of hatred in order to "blacken" a political leader (an especially mediocre one, too) had been appropriated by members of a disempowered group to serve as a mark of pride. Such a transformation differs from taking an enemy's taunt and throwing it back in defiance; this is more akin to rummaging through garbage for a scrap of cultural identity. What did the student's textbook offer as an alternative perspective on black Americans during the period? Passing nods to jazz, the Harlem Renaissance, and yet more sharecropping. How much better to locate a member of the group so close to the center of power that the "truth" of his origins has to be obscured! Tragically, however, the stories of survival and maintaining cultural identity during a hostile time, monumental achievements in themselves, are lost by accepting the standard that the only people worth paying attention to are the ones who occupy the traditional seats of power.[14]

Surely there is ground between the fantasy-history of the Harding myth and the cardboard images of a genial Louis Armstrong or a downtrodden sharecropper. This is not to deny the grim reality that many poor black southerners were forced to confront, but it is a plea to consider how the lives of the ignored and forgotten often provide the clearest insight into the relationships upon which our society chooses to depend. A historical individual remarkable for a strong sense of identity, but not necessarily famous or powerful (like the Alabama farmer Ned Cobb) can speak more directly to students about how the concerns of traditional political history form only a backdrop to the more immediate concerns of maintaining a sense of self in a culture that confuses identity and power.[15] By viewing individuals as they lived at the intersection of their knowledge and power, the barrenness of traditional political history can be replaced with a "pedagogy of cultural politics" in which students are encouraged not only to understand but to act on the realization of their social role.[16] The richness of the past becomes a source of liberation from the impecuniousness of the proper roles and statuses that histories have allotted us.

The new history, therefore, serves the radical function of challenging present power arrangements to justify themselves in terms of the fairness and justice we have proclaimed essential to our well-being. Students are expected not only to master facts or trace lines of historiographical debate; they must also consider how historical relationships relate to the present, with a view toward working for change. In this way, the teacher's, as opposed to the historian's, role is unique: knowledge is not simply to be acquired, or even created, but to be acted upon. The past, therefore, should be allowed to move us in the present so that identities drawn from it are active and not static. Just as the past is made alive with voices once unheard, so we are also better empowered to act in the world we have inherited. Acting in ways that strengthen our society's expectation of justice and opportunity, surely a fundamental (if often ignored) function of public education, requires the conscious selection of those stories which tell of the struggle against injustice and oppression as the ones we will most value. To tell of the experiences oppressed minorities have known—those most dangerous of memories—is to insist that we ask ourselves why the values we honestly espouse have been unrealized in so many lives.

The history which insists on linking past and present cannot bear witness unless it also testifies to the struggles of the past to realize our aspirations. We teach, after all, in anticipation of a better world which we shall never know. If we are to live in community with one another, secure in our ability to create identity, we need the testimony of that cloud of witnesses from the past who have attempted to realize what we also hope to achieve. We do not make the world anew as if all possibilities are unlimited; in thinking we can we risk a false sense of omniscience. We have no guarantee that our follies are any less pernicious than those of an earlier time; the human condition is frail enough that we had best draw upon what inspiration and instruction the past offers us. As our identity is corporate as well as individual, and also rooted in the past, history should inform us of the nature of the ties that have bound us together. Even the most powerful of the ties that make us a people, and not simply a collection of peoples, are not so strong that they can survive neglect. The wrongs we hope to redress require us to revisit the ideals we share and to remember that just as we are capable of doing great wrongs, so, too, do we conceive of noble ends.

It is, in fact, the joining of a radical critique of our histories with a conservative faith in the value of our ideals that gives the past its power to make its claim upon us. Society is defined by humanly ordained arrangements, and the history we choose to tell should serve to dispel the notion that social, political, and economic relationships are the handiwork of arbitrariness and determinism. We do not escape the past by ignoring it, for its influence is not so easily dismissed, yet our identity cannot be contained in narratives we have had no part in telling. Our understandings of the past impel us to act in the present, either to preserve those elements we value or to alter those relationships we deem harmful. However we choose to act—and our education should lead us to act in as conscious a manner as we are able—the past provides the context which defines what is possible.

Having entered the world as the most recent generation, we cannot help but look to the past for some explanation of why we are here. The present age, however, has so completely freed itself from the sense of a universal time that connectedness with the past has been almost lost as well. A single lifetime now encompasses many times, not all of which fit neatly with one another—age, family, career, and faith no longer seem so carefully linked with one another, let alone with grander political seasons, economic cycles, and the approaching millennium.[17] The extreme and idealized views of time hitherto offered by history—that time progresses toward a hopeful future or, for the downtrodden, hardly moves at all—no longer offer convincing descriptions of a world that is in actuality strikingly ambivalent about its future. Not knowing whether we are ushering in heaven or hell—purgatory does not appear to be an option in heralding the future—we hardly know what to ask of the past, except we wonder whether it has any relevance to what we are experiencing now.

Nevertheless, the change in how we perceive time has not been without welcome effects. There is an exhilarating freedom in responding to David Harvey's call that we "challenge the idea of a single and objective sense of time and space against which we can measure the diversity of human conceptions and perceptions."[18] We are freed, for example, from trying to reconcile history as progression toward apotheosis with the human evil we cannot seem to escape. It is, in fact, postmodernity's skepticism toward the spatial concept of hierarchy that allows for alternative histories that move away from the traditionally political. The multitude of past voices that we are more likely to hear today speak to the power of a postmodernist emphasis on diversity. The dictatorships of our times have been proclaimed in the name of modernity's lockstep march into a utopian tomorrow, whereas postmodernity's greater ease with human quirkiness offers hope in an anarchy of voices that may prove more resistant to totalitarianism's goosestep. More importantly, the multitudinous voices newly called forth remind us that a single truth is subject to contestation. That many of these voices have been hushed should give us pause to ask why they have been silenced, and what we have missed by not hearing them.

The problem with abandoning a single sense of time and space, even if it does more accurately describe the world we know, is that we risk losing all sense of equilibrium, which is not necessarily desirous. When we abandon the authoritativeness of one history, all histories become suspect or, as in the case of the Harding myth, equally valid. Insistence upon faithfulness to facts sounds like the defensive action of an embattled status quo interested only in maintaining power. Still, freedom, which depends upon security in community, is different from license, which corrupts such security. If all we want our histories to do is provide a sense of smug self-satisfaction or an image with which to impress our neighbors, we are unlikely to moderate the hyperindividualism that is driving us further apart from each other. Instead of allowing us to engage the present, we allow the past only to amuse our vanity aimlessly, like a specious coat of arms. The hard work of knowing who we are is forsaken for hedonistic abandon in believing that the present is the only reality.

In *The Condition of Postmodernity*, David Harvey describes the "aestheticization of politics," in which aesthetics triumphs over ethics, images prevail over narrative, and simplism replaces life's complexity.[19] Suspicious of authority, we have convinced ourselves that meaning has been corrupted to serve only the interests of the powerful. If all stories are tainted, then it matters little which ones we tell—we might as well make up our own, so long as they provide a brief, if transitory, comfort. At the very time we need the past to provide agency for the present, we have found that recovering a usable past is more difficult. Put another way, the welcome freedom we get from histories that have been narrowly conceived has simultaneously made knowing any convincing account of the past more difficult. Postmodernism has robbed us of the meta-narratives that provided meaning for previous generations. History, argue the authors of *Telling the Truth About History*, in the most extreme postmodernist critique is irrelevant to identity because its dependence upon story and narrative (which, in turn, rest on now-suspect meta-narratives) makes it incapable of being thought of critically.[20]

The irony of postmodernist thought, of course, is that it attempts to substitute its own meta-narrative with the harrowing assertion that the world consists of no more than word games we cannot escape. Postmodernism commits an error common to radical thought of asserting that the past can be ignored by force of will and that the stories we draw from it are merely propaganda for the status quo. While it is possible to find ourselves omitted from the histories we have been given, the past in which we *can* discover our origins remains a wellspring for understanding who we are. Unless we are content to sit amid "a rubble of signifiers," scraping the sores of our alienation with pieces of broken knowledge, we must dare to assert faith that this complex world holds meaning greater than we can know and which nevertheless gives our lives purpose.[21] These are not good times for combining faith in our ability to arrive at meaning that transcends our transitory existence with an acceptance of a limitation to what we can know. Faith and effort, after all, are words with an old-fashioned ring, while paradox and limitation sit uneasily in a culture still desirous of certainty and unlimited possibility. Like a spoiled child, postmodernism would have us believe that we can know nothing if we cannot know everything. Behind the pouting lies the fear of believing that transcendence is possible; indeed, such a concept can not even be conceived of because our words chain us to ourselves.

The ancient art of narrative, however, too strongly satisfies human desire to know for it to be dismissed as irrelevant. From the siege of Troy to television's soap operas, we want to know what happened; most of all, we want to know why. Language, together with music, art, and love, are all we have to express meaning; to moan about how it imprisons us with its closed system of self-reference bespeaks a loss of faith in human creativity. Acknowledging that narrative contains inadequacies (as if it were unlike other human undertakings), is different from denying its power to situate us in the historical processes that bound our existence. Rather than abandon the historian's art, we would do better to explore more fully the predispositions we bring to our work. Whether Edward Isham, to return to an earlier example, brings a stronger message about social alienation or economic struggle (assuming the two can be disengaged from each other) depends in no less degree on the predisposition of the hearer than on the evidence.

Our conversations with the past should include as many people, living and dead, as possible. Urging historians to make better efforts to excite the public's imagination about the past is one thing; perhaps more efficacious is empowering young people to understand creatively how they cannot fully live in the present unless they also live in the past, not with a mournful sense of loss but with a celebratory feeling of discovery of who we are. By making reference outside of themselves, young people are more likely to find security and purpose in a turbulent world. Such a view of education sees history at its best as possessing a power to redeem us by pulling us out of our time to contemplate a past we can never fully know, but that we believe will enable us to affect the present. Only as it combines faith in humankind's ability to continually fashion meaningful explanations of life with the certainty of our limited knowledge (and, as a consequence, the nearly unlimited possibilities for ways to view the past) can education be a source of engagement with the world.

We do not need to explain away the tragic stories of our nation's past; nor do those stories deny the existence of ideals toward which we strive. In fact, the side-by-side existence of the tragic with the ideal suggests—postmodernist criticism to the contrary—a meta-narrative with moving power. The two are inseparably linked, neither subsumed by the other: The tragic points to the unfulfilled ideal, the ideal is a reminder of what we are capable of conceiving. In the cynicism that has resulted from disillusionment in trying to reconcile optimism and progress with the tragic stories that are also our heritage, however, we have concluded that a dull, flat hypocrisy—the postmodernist meta-narrative—best labels the past. Ironically, we insist on a consistency in the past that we would find impossible to live with in the present, where our everyday reality consists of believing simultaneously in contradictory truths. Embracing paradox rather than hypocrisy generates a tension that keeps life dynamic instead of self-defeating.

Just as paradox pervades our lives in the present, it also abounds in our past. The specific paradox central to American history, of course, is slavery and freedom; and, as Edmund S. Morgan has argued, the two not only co-existed, but "grew together, the one supporting the other."[22] Indeed, as the movement toward independence approached, "Virginians may have had a special appreciation of the freedom dear to republicans, because they saw every day what life without it could be like."[23] This is not an apologia for the indefensible, but a willingness to accept both our imperfections and our ability to conceive a higher end. The meta-narrative of paradox, embodying the duality of incompleteness and possibility, spurs us into a historical identity which compels us to act in the present by either justifying or altering the power arrangements by which we live.

A nation which prides itself on classlessness but has known sweatshops; has helped spawn concepts of equality while also having installed separate water fountains; has assimilated into its cultural mainstream diverse millions but also utilized the reservation system—every aspect of our national character related to the issue of power—offers ample opportunity for the exploration of paradox. Never fully realized, the ideals that have defined the most admirable qualities in the communities of our past retain their power to attract our energies, even as we are humbled by how our efforts have fallen short. The multitude of histories we tell of the past foster our personal identities while also returning us to themes we share—of hope and survival—and our expectations for the succeeding generation.

Realization of our common struggle to arrive at meaning in life in an age that has made alienation an art form would be a major accomplishment in itself and might cause us to feel less threatened when we listen to stories that are different from our own. Those stories that move us, however, even as they also discomfort, will require a return to the promises that unite us with questions of why the promises have not been fulfilled. We discover that paradox results not from fortune's whirling wheel but from the unpredictability, uncertainty, and contingency of human action. Our stories are imbued with tension; the values we cherish are weighed against the choices we have made. When the choices weaken the values, we can decide to act or to abandon ourselves to a cultural *Götterdämmerung* where, as the twilight darkens, we might at least be able to perceive how we lost those things we once thought important.

No paradox looms larger than that in which the past can be understood only in light of the present. T. S. Eliot wrote in *Four Quartets*:

> We shall not cease from exploration
> And the end of all our exploring
> Will be to arrive where we started
> And know the place for the first time.[24]

Young people cannot be expected to undertake their arduous exploration unless we help them ask of the past how to return to it. To be useful, their questions will not be of passing antiquarian interest, but will serve to orient them toward their journey. Though their questions may be different from the ones we have asked, they will find that past generations have struggled with the same issues of relationship they must confront. They will understand that they cannot know the past as it was, but only as it speaks to the present. They will discover that the struggle to be heard forges a solidarity between past and present. And therein they will find the courage to live their lives.

Notes

[1] The notes are in the possession of the author. They are dated as follows: Adam A. McNeely, January 3, 1857; T. P. Gillespie, October 25, 1856; and Theos. Allison, August 29, 1857. Henry Mills is listed in the Federal Census of 1860 as an unmarried merchant, aged twenty-nine, living with a four-year-old boy and owning $1,000 of real property. The note writers are not so readily identifiable. Allison, however, does make an appearance in the 1860 Federal Census as a thirty-nine-year-old farmer living near the Granite Hill Post Office and owning real estate valued at $2,000 and personal property valued at $420. Of the five slaves he owned (and who lived in one house), four were women. The fifth, a fourteen-year-old boy, is listed as a fugitive from the state. Eighth Census of the United States, 1860: Iredell County, North Carolina, Population and Slave Schedules.

[2] Berkin et al. 186–93.

[3] Berkin et al. 186.

[4] Berkin et al. 202–3.

[5] T. S. Eliot, "Little Gidding," I, in *Four Quartets* (New York: Harcourt Brace & Company, 1943) 51.

[6] Stanley Aronowitz and Henry A. Giroux, "Schooling, Culture, and Literacy in the Age of Broken Dreams: A Review of Bloom and Hirsch," *Harvard Educational Review* 58 (April 1988): 178.

[7] Eliot, "Burnt Norton," I, 13.

[8] Eliot, "Burnt Norton," II, 16.

[9] Benjamin 254.

[10] Benjamin 252.

[11] Johann-Baptist Metz, "The Future in the Memory of Suffering," in Johann-

Baptist Metz and Jürgen Moltmann, eds., *Faith and the Future: Essays on Theology, Solidarity, and Modernity* (Maryknoll, New York: Orbis Books, 1995) 7–8.

[12] Paulo Freire asserts, "Liberation is praxis, the action and reflection of man upon their world in order to transform it." Paulo Freire, *Pedagogy of the Oppressed* (New York: Continuum Publishing Company, 1970) 229–30.

[13] Francis Russell, *The Shadow of Blooming Grove: Warren G. Harding in His Times* (New York: McGraw-Hill Book Company, 1968) 530.

[14] In *Trouble in Mind: Black Southerners in the Age of Jim Crow* (New York: Alfred A. Knopf, 1998), Leon F. Litwack counters the cardboard images I describe in the text with stories of survival and identity "waged over the meaning of freedom." Litwack xviii.

[15] Theodore Rosengarten, *All God's Dangers: The Life of Nate Shaw* (New York: Alfred A. Knopf, 1974). Nate Shaw was the fictitious name of Ned Cobb (1885–1973).

[16] Henry A. Giroux, "Critical Pedagogy, Cultural Politics, and the Discourse of Experience," in James R. Gress and David E. Purpel, eds., *Curriculum: An Introduction to the Field* (Berkeley, California: McCutchan Publishing Corporation, 1988) 442.

[17] David Harvey, *The Condition of Postmodernity: An Enquiry into the Origins of Cultural Change* (New York: Basil Blackwell Ltd., 1989) 327.

[18] Harvey 327.

[19] See especially Harvey 351–5.

[20] Appleby et al. 233.

[21] "But in challenging all consensual standards of truth and justice, of ethics, and meaning, and in pursuing the dissolution of all narratives and meta-theories into a diffuse universe of language games, deconstructionism ended up, in spite of the best intentions of its more radical practitioners, by reducing knowledge and meaning to a rubble of signifiers." Harvey 351.

[22] Edmund S. Morgan, *American Slavery, American Freedom: The Ordeal of Colonial Virginia* (New York: W. W. Norton & Company, Inc., 1975) 6.

[23] Morgan 376.

[24] Eliot, "Little Gidding," V, 59.

Chapter 4

The Limits of Enlightenment

"Living history" is a term used by those who enjoy portraying the past through costume and recreation of historical events and periods. Much can be learned about the Revolutionary War, for example, by actually toting a heavy, flintlock musket and drilling with it so as to fire four rounds in a minute's time, as was expected of well-trained Continental soldiers. Working like an automaton, one grows accustomed to the gun's noise, which is less concussive to the person firing the weapon than it is to the cringing bystander; and to the smoke, which envelopes the musketmen in a fog reeking of sulfur. The drill's effect is impressive: a pleasing sense of coordination within the squad, the rumbling noise that echoes across a rolling field, the strangely ethereal feeling of firing within a bank of clouds. Both audience and participant leave satisfied that the past has been convincingly recreated.

There is, of course, much that has escaped us in our attempt to recapture the past. Unavailable to us are numerous details. The wool used in newly fashioned coats, for example, lacks the fineness to be left raw-edged, without a hem, unlike surviving originals.[1] While we can command a host of particulars concerning an eighteenth-century army's appearance, we really do not know how closely our composite image corresponds to that which really existed in a given time and place. More glaring is that a few dozen men cannot hope to recreate the effect of an army numbering in the hundreds, struggling to maneuver over unfamiliar terrain in conditions far removed from the parade ground. What most lends an air of untruthfulness to this scene, however—in spite of our best efforts to arrive at authenticity—is how the proceedings are framed with an audience which does not really expect to see blood or hunger or disease or suffering of the participants. The event is clearly demarcated in time. While both audience and participant may be thrilled by their experience, no one lives in fear of the direction it might take or the uncertainty of how it will conclude. The reality is illusory and dissipates as quickly and harmlessly as the gunpowder's smoke.

This trivial illustration serves as a metaphor for more serious, equally misguided efforts to know original intent, an indication of how uncertain we are in our own judgment, as evidenced in forums that include the performance of classical music on "authentic" instruments and debates over how the Supreme Court should arrive at its decisions. All such attempts to arrive at new/old understandings will come to frustration, however, if we fail to remember that we cannot separate ourselves from our times. We can no more read the Constitution in the way the Founding Fathers did, removed from them as we are by two centuries of political experience, than we can hear Mozart the way his Viennese audience did. One might even argue that the postmodern critique of the function of knowledge explains more about the supercilious belief that the experience of one age can be swapped for another than the desire for authenticity does.

The living history reenactment suggests several ways in which our knowledge of the past is always circumscribed by constraints that concern the past itself as well as ones regarding us. The simplest limitation of our knowledge is that too many facts about the past elude us. Time acts as the great eraser of memory, leaving us to search for what may be irretrievably lost. Even so, this limitation is hardly the most severe one confronting our quest to know the past, despite the attention it popularly receives every time a new and unforeseen discovery about the past is announced.[2] Had we at our disposal all possible facts, we would still be left with the task of deciding their meaning, an undertaking that varies in difficulty with the quantity of information available, but which is, nevertheless, more difficult than gathering evidence. The difficulty lies primarily in trying to think like those who lived on the opposite side of the events we are studying who had experiences and perspectives different from our own. When we consider Robert Darnton's observation that "other people are other," we realize how the historian must tease "the meaning inscribed by contemporaries in whatever survives of their vision of the world."[3] Our experience in this world, however, circumscribes what we can know of an "other" one. To return to an earlier example, Mozart sounds different—even when played faithfully in the style he would have approved of and on the instruments he knew (two centuries of use or neglect notwithstanding)—to the ears that have also heard Stravinsky, not to mention rock-and-roll. This means we can only surmise how the former's music sounded before the experience of the latter. Our knowledge is of the second-hand kind, as we always remain conscious of our status as outsiders looking through the windows of a salon at individuals who cannot return our gaze.

Evidence and interpretation are the purview of the historian. All of us—teacher and historian included—should consider our own restraints to what we can know. Just as past and present exist only in relationship to each other, so we cannot understand the stories we recover without knowing our own stories, in particular those stories whose meanings motivate us. The past does not lie still, awaiting our discovery; instead, it expects "an agent who actively molds how the past is to be seen."[4] Our agency flows from our identity, and it sensitizes us to what we are able to hear and what we want to ask of the past. Joyce Appleby and her colleagues describe the awareness of this "interactive relationship" as a "practical realism," which requires the teacher/historian to maintain as much faithfulness to facts as possible by acknowledging the values we bring to historical inquiry.[5]

The human condition guarantees that our efforts to know ourselves will be flawed. The task has not gotten any easier since Socrates's day. Worse still would be the attempt to mitigate our struggle by deluding ourselves that nothing more is required than to be more inclusive of the stories of others on the assumption that we are acting with their best interests at heart. We are not free agents; if we are alienated from one another, we also bind together by sharing this sense of loss. The effect of our common estrangement is to hamper what any one individual feels empowered to do. Simply deciding by oneself to be more inclusive of other's stories, however admirable, will not do because of the broader and overpowering sense that nothing we attempt will make much difference. If we fail to address alienation on the societal level, we will be frustrated in witnessing the efforts of no more than a few rare individuals willing to risk their own social standing by displaying the fortitude to buck the mood of the culture.

Michael Lerner used the term "surplus powerlessness" to describe these "debilitating psychological effects of oppression and the internalization of cruelty."[6] Rather than attempt to change the world, Lerner argues, we succumb to the temptation to adapt ourselves to it. More than just accepting the culture's "common sense," Lerner argues that surplus powerlessness "is also intertwined with a complex set of feelings about oneself."[7] We are able to believe that whatever happens to us is deserved, hence the sense of futility we feel about trying to change the world.

Lerner locates the source of much of this powerlessness in the Jewish experience as a subjected and dispersed people, but we can also find surplus powerlessness at work in all of us for another reason, as well.[8] The temptation to yield to the present arrangement of power is a particularly alluring one, for, as Michel Foucault has observed, power is "a productive network that runs through the whole social body," where "it traverses and produces things, it induces pleasure, forms knowledge, produces discourse."[9] Power, then, is not simply a repressive thing imposed from on high; it is the very framework of our existence.

So we reach the great divide in contemporary existence. Modernism, with its roots in the Enlightenment's rational inquiry and denial that the past has any claim on the present, stands before the heap of progress' broken promises, opposite the call of a spiritual ethos to transcend the present world in order to change it with the power of what Foucault described as the "insurrection of subjected knowledges."[10] The call of transcendence is spiritual because we are asked not to depend solely on experiences and knowledge of the present, but to hear, sometimes for the first time, the cry for justice from the voices of the past. At the same time, we do not surrender ourselves to a view of the past that renders us the helpless products of its historicism, but we recognize that, in their own fashion, others have been where we now are, struggling with issues that are never finally resolved. The past, then, is too rich for a shallow, two-dimensional triumphalism, and we depend upon the resourcefulness and rigorousness of historical research to illuminate the variety of possibilities for understanding the present. Our spiritual ethos makes urgent this need to know.

"The [Christian] memory of suffering . . . brings a new moral imagination into political life, a new vision of others' suffering that should mature into a generous, uncalculating partisanship on behalf of the weak and unrepresented," asserts Johann-Baptist Metz.[11] We who teach must decide if we will serve an end higher than ourselves. By listening to those whom the rest of society has decided not to hear, we have made a decision to challenge the existing arrangement of power. For the teacher motivated by Christian precept, the motivating model is of the Jesus who outraged the established order by befriending the sinner and comforting the outcast while directing his wrath toward the hypocrisy of the powerful who claimed to love God while not recognizing Him in their neighbor. This model is a dangerous one because it is subversive and, therefore, not the way our culture usually recognizes an individual's religious orientation. Jesus, after all, was crucified because he insisted on an active faith that transformed the world in ways that brought it closer to a Kingdom in which the first should be last.

While we are quick to welcome the Christ who comforts the lowly with an assurance of future glory, we are less inclined to recognize how his claim to transform life in the present is based on the belief—rooted in Jewish theology—that because we are created in the image of God, our worth is intrinsic and not something to be achieved. Our task is to realize this sense of worth by insisting that the stories we most value return us to an examination of our claims to a just and fair society. What we will discover in these stories is that both oppressor and oppressed reside in each of us.[12] As flawed creatures, perfect justice and fairness will always elude us. Peter's denial that he knew Jesus was as earnest as his avowal to follow him even to death had been shortly before. To the extent of our failure to realize this utopia, we act—perhaps unintentionally and regretfully—as oppressor.

At the same time, we have no choice but to act out of our blemished past. Rarely are we as individuals able to live out our perfect dreams and aspirations, despite whatever material advantages we may possess. In the mystery of our existence we conceive of ends higher than we can achieve, nevertheless burdened if we hope to maintain our humanity, with the responsibility to pursue them. "To remember the reality of oppression in the lives of people and to value those lives," affirms Sharon Welch, "is to be saved from the luxury of hopelessness."[13] It is at this point that the tension between religious conviction and rational enlightenment is held in balance. The memory of the suffering of Christ impels us to delve into the historical record for the subjugated and forgotten stories that retain their power to move us. We dare to expect transcendence in the manner that the word has been defined by Michael Lerner: "Transcendence is not transcending *this* world, but rather our ability to bring more fully into being *in* this world aspects of ourselves and aspects of reality that surround us but to which we have become tone deaf."[14] We have accomplished this goal in material ways, thinking that the material would in and of itself take care of the spiritual. Public education in particular has succumbed to the fallacy that conflates prosperity with a vibrant community, dulling us to the idea that the unrestrained pursuit of the former may actually subvert the latter.

To be genuinely concerned with the education of our youth, the teacher/historian cannot assume that it is possible for scholarship to remain both relevant and above the fray of political interests contending for domination in society. Perhaps no scholar has employed such riotous imagery to describe the folly of an insular and unrestrained pursuit of history as the Oxford cleric Robert Burton in *The Anatomy of Melancholy* (1621):

> Your supercilious criticks, grammatical triflers, notemakers, curious antiquaries, find out all the ruins of wit, gutters of folly, amongst the rubbish of old writers; and what they take they spoil, all fools with them that cannot find fault; they correct others, & are hot in a cold cause, puzzle themselves to find out how many streets in Rome, houses, gates, towers, Homer's country, Aeneas's mother, Niobe's daughters, whether Sappho was a public woman? which came first, the egg or the hen? &c & other things which you would try to forget if you ever knew them, as Seneca holds; . . . which for the present for an historian to relate . . . is very ridiculous, is to them most precious elaborate stuff, they admired for it, and as proud, as triumphant in the mean time for this discovery, as if they had won a city, or conquered a province; as rich as if they had found a mine of gold ore.[15]

Burton makes plain his attitude that the intellectual's labor is pointless—"mad," or "melancholic," to use his phraseology—if it bears no relation to present-day concerns.[16] "Is not he mad that draws lines with Archimedes, whilst his house is ransacked, and his city besieged, when the whole world is in combustion, or we whilst our souls are in danger . . . . to spend our time in toys, idle questions, and things of no worth?"[17]

We stand in danger today of losing both our souls and our belief that what we know can make for a more just society by acquiescing to relationships that tolerate the inequities dividing and separating us. Ultimately, soul and mind are joined, which means that any threat to one endangers the other. When we refuse to acknowledge humankind's suffering, our role in extending it, and our ability to challenge it, we cast our wizened souls into the darkness, confessing that the only purpose of knowledge is to perpetuate our own power. We ignore the knowledge of others, which means that we also disregard anyone not like us. Instead of aspiring to liberate the captive, we search for ways to be more secure in our role as oppressor, desperately hoping that we are able to live out our days and die peacefully in our beds.

"Whatever," reads the bumper sticker of our times—a frankly dispiriting admission that none of our stories matter much because all of them lack the power to direct our lives in meaningful ways.

We are too cynical to believe the stories told to us by authorities and we lack the faith that anyone else's stories can change anything. We have at our disposal, however, memory that is dangerous, if we can only summon the courage to give it voice. What is required of us is a faith that is not to believe in the unseen, but one that—as Sharon Welch has observed—"is a stance of being, an acceptance of risk and openness, an affirmation of both the importance of human life (its dimension of ultimate significance) and the refusal to collapse that ultimacy into a static given, identifying it as definitively achieved in some concrete medium of its manifestation."[18] This faith is pragmatic: However we individually ascribe the source of our motivation, we must collectively insist on results that are tangible while simultaneously remembering that the past which informs also circumscribes. Our victories will be hard-won yet incomplete, life-changing yet never permanently secure.

Faith in transcendence is the vehicle that shuttles between human enlightenment and spiritual insight. Enlightenment allows for a reconstruction of the past in ways that speak to the identity of the present. It insists on fidelity to the facts as best they can be recovered and understood, while not only acknowledging the agency we bring to the making of history but also critically analyzing how our agency has been used to fashion an understanding of who we are. It is simplistic to claim knowledge for its own sake; we expect that what we know will make a difference in how we live (an assertion with both good and evil ramifications). Truth as the historian would understand it is provisional and subject to revision as the past reveals more of itself and both we and our times change to allow the past to be seen in different lights. We carry with us as a lodestone, however, faith that we can transcend the world as we know it with the world as we would have it.

Our research offices and classrooms will remain no more than the habitations of Burton's grammatical triflers and notemakers if we do not make explicit which stories we most want to hear and to tell. Choosing those stories is not easy; life abounds with enough pain for all of us to share, and each identity, of course, is a prized possession to be nurtured. Perhaps, then, there is a lesson here for our nation's public education: A good share of what students learn should be directed by them in order to fulfill their personal need for rooting their own being in time and space. Without historical consciousness, individuals are left to endure alone the vicissitudes of the present, unaware of the ties that join them to others and to the decisions that have shaped their lives. This precept rests on the notion of the individual's intrinsic worth and suggests a pedagogical model in which teachers are responsible for helping students with the techniques of historical research, then getting out of the way. Without care, however, we might quickly find ourselves back at the "whatever" attitude in which any identity—based on any slipshod story—is acceptable, even apart from the question of being honest about the facts. Identities are not part of a wardrobe, to be suited to whatever personal statement we may wish to make. Understanding one's identity is arduous, even painful, and the labor of a lifetime, both in and out of the classroom.

Such an individual approach to learning, however, no matter how honest, will support our society only so far. As we flourish or perish by the strength of our sense of community, we need to summon the fortitude required to persevere, whatever the limitations on our ability to know, in recovering the stories that return us to a social contract of life lived free from want and fear. We fail, not when we are forced to admit that transcending our present existence constantly eludes us, but when we do not use the truth we have. Principal among what we can claim as truth is the ability to make our moralism honest by molding a past that is as rich, complex, and paradoxical as the present. To do less is to deny too many of the voices of the dead, which is hardly different from shunting those of the living.

How does the teacher/historian adapt to a role that flies in the face of so much that public education is about these days? Robert Burton concluded that the world was filled with "such shifting, lying, cogging, plotting, counter-plotting, temporizing, flattering, cozening, dissembling, that of necessity one must highly offend God, if he be comfortable to the world, . . . or else live in contempt, disgrace, and misery."[19] I know of no more difficult question, for teaching as a *profession* in the earliest meaning of the word—a public acknowledgment of belief—is impatient with temporizing. It helps to know that the experience of teaching allows for teachers to learn and grow alongside their students, and to be of help even when they are unsure of what to do. Ultimately, however, the countless small decisions of daily existence color a lifetime, and, in the end, we stand alone with the effects of our choices. We will face that time with greater ease knowing that we recognized our limitations, did our best within them, and looked for ways to push them back.

Knowing limits is perhaps the one eternal, universal human

lesson, if one may dare to use such words in a postmodernist world. Foucault wrote of a life that is "conceived as an attitude, an ethos, a philosophical life in which the critique of what we are is at one and the same time the historical analysis of the limits that are imposed on us and an experiment with the possibility of going beyond them."[20] Admitting to the limits of our knowledge is not surrendering to despair; it is, rather, a precondition for attempting to go beyond them. We are relieved of the burden of an unobtainable omniscience because we understand that we live only in reference to a specific past which cannot be denied. We know our faults, prejudices, and idiosyncrasies; recognizing them, we can purposely contend with them. We are also more likely to have a realistic notion of what is possible, both at our best and worst. We are not, however, permitted the luxury of relinquishing our duty to test those limits. The goals toward which we strive are not abstract; they are based on what we have been able to conceive and accomplish in our past. If we allow ourselves to be intoxicated by the postmodernist endeavor of denying the existence of any meaning apart from the culture's arrangement of power—and thereby succumb to a feeling of impotence at effecting change—we will have inadvertently given triumph to the seats of power we would challenge.

The search for a usable past begins and ends with a meditation on family history. Sometime in the 1850s, Nathan Wesley Culclasure and his wife Sarah sat for their photographs in Orangeburg, South Carolina. The photographs came into my branch of the family through the scanty collection of personal papers left by a great-aunt. She had apparently misidentified the couple, giving them the names of her parents—their children—a blatant error considering his silk cravat and frock coat and her lace gloves and chignon. This old, spinster great-aunt, as I had known her, was absorbed with the family's history to the extent that in her declining years she mailed to me, along with the postage stamps she had clipped for my collection, the hokum of commercial genealogies she had obtained, convinced of their explanation of the family name. Who knows?—She was just as likely to have bought the photographs—identified only by the town where they were made—at a flea market, penciling on the back the names of the people she wanted to see in them. Few facts, much room for speculation.

I think the photographs are of family ancestors, however, and I get the strangest feeling looking at the one I think was Nathan

Wesley. There, except for the pomaded hair and tall, stiff shirt collar, sits my brother, or my father, as a young man. It is hard to say exactly what makes the resemblance so strong—the soft chin, perhaps, or the wistful look of the deep-set, lightly colored eyes. Considering the physical features, one wonders whether other, less easily detected characteristics of personality could also be preserved across so much time. What qualities, for example, were required of a slaveholder, and were such qualities inheritable? This man, after all, lived at a time when the institution was under furious attack. Surely his feelings were complex, even contradictory, just as ours are in issues both related to and unconnected with race. Looking at the incongruous combination of an almost shy, youthful visage and his clenched, gloved, and authoritative hand, it is easy to imagine the tentativeness with which he might have faced his future. And what of Sarah, his wife: Did her role as mistress of the household require of her characteristics that had to be carefully cultivated because they were so unnatural, or do humans, when provided the opportunity, easily tend toward tyranny? Imagining, however, is all we can do as we look at the faded photographs, since, except for their appearances in census reports and the sites of their graves, the couple left no other tangible records of their existence.

The fact of the photographs' existence is clear enough; their identity is slightly less certain. What one sees in them may be as much the result of looking inward as outward. Entwined in this family are many stories that are untold and, to a degree, unknowable. Nevertheless, they are stories that can be partially reclaimed: a young couple separated by war, an extended family (at least allegorically), separated by race; an existence dependent on the pain visited upon others who were swept up in unimaginable fury; the legacy of two families, former masters and freedmen, consciously sharing little more than their surname. The stories' endings are frayed; they lack the sense of a triumphant march into the future. They are also painful, which, for a people characterized by optimism, is an unwelcome quality. So painful are they, in fact, that remembering them in terms of how equality, opportunity, fairness, and justice are defined and practiced today makes them dangerous threats to the arrangements of power in the present. That is all the more reason for telling them, for, without stories like these to make us consider the choices we have made, we will be too easily convinced that impersonal historical forces are beyond our ability to direct. Had we come to this conclusion, we would have abandoned the agency that makes us human. We would have also lost any morally justifiable reason to teach.

Notes

[1] See, for example, the raw-edged wool broadcloth frock coat (1983–228) illustrated in Linda Baumgarten, *Eighteenth-Century Clothing at Williamsburg* (Williamsburg, VA: Colonial Williamsburg Foundation, 1986) 64.

[2] This is not to deny the way an unexpected historical find can transform our understanding of an earlier era. For one recent and well-publicized example, the discovery in Egypt of the tombs of Ramesses II's sons, see Douglas Preston, "All the King's Sons," *The New Yorker* 22 January 1996: 44–59.

[3] Robert Darnton, *The Great Cat Massacre* (New York: Random House, 1985) 4–5.

[4] Appleby et al. 249.

[5] Appleby et al. 247, 261.

[6] Michael Lerner, *Jewish Renewal: A Path to Healing and Transformation* (New York: G. P. Putnam's Sons, 1994) 111.

[7] Lerner 112.

[8] Lerner 316–7.

[9] Michel Foucault, *Power/Knowledge: Selected Interviews and Other Writings, 1972–1977* (New York: Pantheon Books, 1980) 119.

[10] Foucault 81.

[11] Metz 15.

[12] For an example of someone moved by a sense of being both oppressor and oppressed, see Sharon D. Welch, *Communities of Resistance and Solidarity: A Feminist Theology of Liberation* (Maryknoll, New York: Orbis Books, 1985) ix–x.

[13] Welch 90.

[14] Lerner 29.

[15] Robert Burton, "Democritus to the Reader," in *The Anatomy of Melancholy* (New York: Farrar & Rinehart, 1927) 95–6.

[16] Burton also recognized how a scholar must depend too often on the support of the powerful in order to make his own existence economically viable, anticipating the more sinister observation Aronowitz and Giroux cited earlier. "So they [scholars] prostitute themselves, as fiddlers or mercenary tradesmen, to serve great men's turns for a small reward." Burton 265.

[17] Burton 96.

[18] Welch 78.

[19] Burton 53.

[20] Michel Foucault, "What Is Enlightenment?," in Paul Rabinow, ed., *The Foucault Reader* (New York: Pantheon, 1984) 50.

PART II

From Theory to Practice

Chapter 5

The Past I Have Known

To say that through some of my students I have known Edward Isham—furiously ranging across his landscape—and his daughter Margaret Bone—orphaned and stigmatized even as an infant—causes the historian in me to part ways with the teacher. My scholarship is uncomfortable with the assumption that the past can be known in so surreal a way; the past is too strange, too far removed from us to be recognized in the present. The poor may be with us still, but not the same poor, and to pretend otherwise flattens the past to the point where it loses its distinctiveness. Teaching by such misplaced lights only reinforces the commonly held conviction that the past has nothing to say to us that cannot be learned from today's soap opera. Worse than simply neglecting the past, we pretend to know it by unthinkingly imposing upon it a modern world view.

Even so, if the historian leaves he does not go far. He dawdles along the sidewalk a short distance behind, pretending to be looking through the gate of a neglected cemetery, but still keeping the teacher in view, as if afraid of being left alone. If the teacher depends upon the historian for a sensitivity to the peculiarities of the past and a richness of learning not often encountered in the classroom, the historian looks to the teacher as someone who must fashion the stories with which to inspire students desiring to find their own voices. It is a variation on the Faust theme: The historian's learning does him little good if he lacks an audience of listeners—an up-close, sometimes restless, often inquisitive, always critical audience who can react to what they hear either by rejecting it or demanding more, maybe even remaking the stories into their own in the process.

It requires considerable give-and-take to accommodate within one person the passions of both the teacher and the historian; witness its rarity by the breathlessness which accompanies its discovery by the public. When I began to teach, newly graduated from a college where I had worked much harder in my historical studies than in the pedagogical courses, I understood teaching to be a means of enlightening my students—indeed, overwhelming them—with the power of my learning, as if its brilliance could awe them into an appreciation of history. Needless to say, the students did not sit in my presence like an aboriginal people gathered around the silver fuselage of a wrecked airplane. And what if they had? My growth as well as theirs would have been stunted because none of us had entered what Jo Anne Pagano terms the "cultural conversation" where the "understanding of ourselves and our communities" occurs.[1] I had yet to learn how "to tell our stories in conversation with the stories we are told."[2] Like wreckage on a beach, my learning lay useless, without value except as an object of unthinking worship.

During that trying time I learned what at first seemed no more than enlightened self-interest: I had to do something different to stave off my own boredom. No one, including me, cared what I knew. For the students, my knowledge of the past was no more interesting than yesterday's cafeteria lunch, except that—and this realization was as real as it was horrible—I had the power to serve it again and again. As a new teacher, I worried more about mastering subject content, so as not to be caught by my students in an embarrassing slip of fact, than I did in getting to know who they were. Carried away with the belief that I could ride my history hobbyhorse without pause, I lost my audience before I realized it. In wondering where my students' attention went I could not help but ask who they were. Once I started asking, the atmospherics of the classroom slowly changed. If the students had stopped listening to me, I began listening to them, and I quickly learned not only something of who they were, but who I was as well. What should have been self-evident grew clearer: My own bookish, somewhat solitary past had kept me from knowing much about those I was supposed to be teaching.

Did it matter whether I could identify these young people in ways more significant than memorizing their nicknames? It was certainly fun to abandon a formal lesson plan and allow a conversation to begin without having to reach a predetermined objective drawn from the standard course of study, although my early fear that a principal might observe an inattentive class and conclude I could not "maintain control" was being replaced with the worry that I might now be failing to keep students "on task." I discovered that nothing is harder to explain to an outsider than raucous laughter coming from inside the classroom.

I also realized that not everyone was like me. Some of my students possessed wealth beyond any I was ever likely to know, but more striking was how these individuals accounted for their status. The confidence they bore and the ease with which they related to me and their peers was the manifestation of a belief that hard work was the simple and only ingredient required for making a successful life. And they were willing to work hard (despite their frequently well-deserved, goofball image dependent on parental intervention to set things right) because school worked for them. They were the class officers, the yearbook superlatives, and, to be honest, the students I most enjoyed being around. They had it made, but they did not have a clue why their less fortunate peers failed to share their enjoyment of high school and its promise of an even more exciting future. "Everyone has the same chance," I often heard them say, "you just have to take advantage of your opportunities." Maybe, I thought. Then again, I was working pretty hard myself and where was it taking me? I found myself settling into one of those professions which is constantly described in terms of its intangible rewards, a giveaway that the tangible ones are scarce.

The correlation between hard work and the good life, to the extent that it could be measured in outward ways, seemed tenuous. Even for these young people, life evidenced its cruel contradictions, as I realized when their stories of privilege came to be interspersed with more somber hints of drug abuse, eating disorders, parental divorce, or the wanton behavior—signs of boredom or a lack of direction?—that they willingly associated with events like spring break. Theirs was the good life, and it seemed to me that they did not have sense enough to appreciate it.

What makes public school so distinctive, of course, is the mixture of students with differing backgrounds that is encountered even in one classroom, despite the tendencies of academic tracking to isolate dissimilar groups of students from one another. So I learned about other students, like those who teased each other for receiving food stamps or having relatives who lived in rural hinterlands or urban ghettoes. There were students whose skin color was the same as mine, but who spoke with "country" accents that I had always associated with lifestyles suited to *Tobacco Road*. All these voices were louder and harsher than those to which I was accustomed.

For a long time, I did not know how to respond to the students who were African-American. The desegregation that occurred in my youth was neither terribly traumatic nor an experience that brought me much meaningful contact with African-Americans.

Although my family lived in a modest neighborhood built early in the post–World War II suburban boom, I enjoyed sufficient acceptance by my peers at school to associate with the more affluent. For most of my childhood, the idea "African-American"—and my family was polite enough to say "black" and to frown on racial jokes—had limited meaning. It included only the maid beloved by children at the elementary school I attended; the lone adolescent in junior high who dressed like we did, and because he was not perceived as a threat, was affably tolerated; and the vague masses whose separate entrance into the movie theater my mother was loath to explain. Because they were alternately heartbreaking and frightening, television images failed to resolve my ambivalence. The friends and others I remember from high school are all white, while in college the only classmates and professors of color I knew were either African or West Indian. Only in part-time work did I come to know well individuals who were black southerners; I liked them, but always self-consciously. Now that I was a teacher, however, I had no choice but to interact with students who were not only different, but recognized their difference from me and—if I had only known—also wondered what to make of it all.

There were other students in my classes. It seemed that I taught an endless stream of siblings and relatives of a large family of Lumbee Indians, which meant that not only did I grow uncomfortable in talking about the institution of slavery, I could not even begin a consideration of the European settlement in the Americas without wondering what was left publicly unsaid but might be screaming inside one of my student's minds.

Every class period seemed to bring another experience beyond my own. I knew the children of mill workers, children who seemed to know more than I did about how demanding work could be. Years of survival in the educational bureaucracy of public education were required before I felt that I could counter the hard view of work some of these young people brought to class with a comparable one, and, even then, I realized how much better off I was. One of the most dramatic encounters, however, came with someone who had not known the work world. She was the daughter of a rabbi for whom the Holocaust was a real horror, and her family introduced me to both a survivor of the camps and a veteran who had participated in one of the camp liberations.

With so many different students, I grew increasingly aware of how much my life differed from theirs. Not only had much of my knowledge been born of my passion for books and classical music,

I also understood that my exposure to books and classical music marked me as a member of a social class as much as it distinguished me as an individual. Here in my classes were voices and stories different from mine, different from anything I had been able to imagine. And I discovered that I liked talking with my students. To my surprise, they were also eager—within the context of the not infrequently awkward relationship between grown teacher and adolescent student—to talk with me, although perhaps their curiosity was akin to interviewing an approachable alien from another planet.

The classroom was beginning to teach me what would later be reinforced with more formal study: "The true starting point of history," as John Dewey expressed it, "is always some present situation with its problems."[3] Even so, any present situation I might choose seemed too far removed from too many students' experiences to afford a good beginning point for venturing into the past. In fact, what was most signal in the attitude of these young people was their belief that none of the history they had ever studied in school was more than dead stuff in need of proper burial. A pedagogy that had failed to show how "this past is the history of the present," with all its complex social arrangements, only furthered an adolescent tendency to think that the present was too unique to benefit from reference to the past.[4] At first, I could only curse the dullness of teachers who had blunted their students' (and most likely their own) edge of curiosity. Only after much more experience would I wonder if robbing history of its ability to attune us to the past fostered a consequence that some might find desirable; namely, to keep silent the voices that made us uncomfortable.

For me, as a teacher, the greatest challenge had now come. In the face of so many competing stories, did I really believe that the ones I brought forth—both my own and the historical ones with which I had surrounded myself—were of value? Shuffling them off and acquiescing to the students' desire to let the dead bury their dead, though easy, would force me to deny part of my own identity while asserting their worthiness might require more nerve than I possessed. While I could not but recognize that my students made a fair demand in knowing how anything we studied related to them, I also could not let go of the stories I wanted to tell and believed should be shared, even if I could not instantly show their pertinence. One choice entailed continuous frustration with the students while the other encouraged resentment for having given up something I valued.

What ensued, without being so clearly stated, was a time of negotiation between me and my students that resulted in all of us sharing something of who we were. I had come of age working at a national park that commemorated the site of a Revolutionary War battle and where, as my youth gave way to adulthood, I came to be greatly affected by that era's mixture of idealism and imperfectly realized promise. I drew meaning from the popular music of the Revolution. I liked its sturdy, straightforward sense of struggle and hopefulness, and it was an easy affection because it had been a real part of many of the interpretive programs in which I participated. Now that I was teaching in the classroom, however, I understood that if I wanted students to hear this era's music meaningfully I would have to connect it with something they had experienced and valued. So I would bring my music to class and invite students to bring theirs. We would exchange printed copies of the lyrics and begin to listen, a fun but crude exercise that was more meaningful if we knew beforehand that the music I would play possessed common themes: messages of liberty and self-determination, love and loss. Asking students if the music they liked offered similar ideas resulted in fruitful conversation; some themes could be readily appreciated while others carried strange import that the students did not understand. Best of all, such a simple exercise allowed me to tell the stories I knew best and also to listen to what these young people had to say about things they were interested in. Talking with them promoted a sense of community, perhaps no more than a fleeting semblance of community in a vaguely hostile environment outside the classroom that continued to insist upon measurable achievement and perfunctory schooling. Even so, there were moments when the past, replete like us with its graces and its blemishes, moved among us as surely as if it, too, had been assigned a seat.

In *Exiles and Communities: Teaching in the Patriarchal Wilderness*, Jo Anne Pagano describes what makes possible such an evanescent moment:

> To have an open mind is to confront, willingly and authentically, the other's story, to enter the story as dialogue. Open-minded persons *claim* their own knowledge and tell their own stories, but they are always mindful of the fact that they may not change minds. Open-minded persons do not merely tolerate other voices; they listen and respond.[5]

Only afterward did I appreciate that what I had regarded as little more than a technique for effective teaching had evolved into a way of humanizing what is in so many ways a dehumanizing place to work. And what I found was not simply that my teaching was less burdensome to me (not to mention to the students), but that together we had much to learn about our world, past and present. For the first time, we were less ready, if only slightly, to dispute without thinking that which each had to say; now, at least for a time, we listened and asked what we meant.

"Making history means form-giving and meaning-giving," asserts Gerda Lerner.[6] Without form and meaning bestowed by us, the past is silent. Because form and meaning are inherent and inescapable when we talk of the past, failing to articulate them leaves us at the mercy of unconsidered tradition and unexamined authority. Our concern, therefore, is in *what* form and with *which* meaning should we imbue the past.

How we answer this question results not in philosophical abstraction but in an orientation that directly informs our practices as a teacher. And as teachers, our practices cannot be easily separated from our relationships with students, as Deborah P. Britzman observes:

> [S]tudents do not simply absorb cultural authority. They mediate it, refuse it, or refashion it with their own significance. This approach to school knowledge recognizes the context in which knowledge is produced and interpreted and attends to the subjective investments of those who produce it.[7]

As public education acquiesces to demands that achievement be standardized and measurable, we increasingly teach in the detestable ways that are too familiar to burned-out teachers and worn-out students, imposing as we do fragmented bits of knowledge stripped of their context, sheared of their relationships, and devoid of all vibrancy.

We will not hear the past if students and teachers do not listen to each other in the present. Arriving at meaning requires conversation, which recognizes that our identities—individual and societal—depend upon relationships with each other. In this sense should learning be concrete, anchored in the realities of lived experience. "Our discussion of justice, freedom, empathy, commitment, and care may help pass the time," Jo Anne Pagano notes, "they may even be diverting, but they are attached neither to objects nor experience."[8]

There comes a point, of course, when the teacher must leave theorizing about how to teach students for the drawing up of next week's lesson plans. In teaching about the past, I have tried to adhere to five basic precepts. This number contains no Pythagorean significance but does seem to me to neatly embrace the essence of good history teaching:

1. *History must be tangible.* This precept has two implications. First, the "stuff" of history—its artifacts, physical and cultural—is an important tool for teaching. Second, even abstractions like "intellectual" history, not usually understood through the interpretation of artifacts, should be grounded in real, concrete terms.

2. *History is personal.* The temptation to talk of great historical forces is the temptation of hubris. Although at times we may be at a loss to describe causation, history is best perceived as affecting people, both famous and obscure, and the ways in which they helped direct events.

3. *History is narrative.* While a quantitative approach to the past can be invaluable, it should not replace the teacher's role as storyteller. As storytellers, we assume a role and fill a need that is at least as old as Homer and one that educators, like the broader culture, disparage as they push for greater "accountability" and standardized assessment.

4. *History is fluid.* It is not the dry, dead stuff of antiquarians. Instead, its meaning flows back and forth into the present, everchanging its appearance as the present's perspective changes.

5. *History requires human agency.* Historical events are the results of human decisions and are not determined by ineluctable forces, causes, or laws governing human behavior. Decisions made one way, therefore, could have been made another way, and resulting consequences are no less significant because they were unforeseen or unknowable.

The following classroom examples attempt to illuminate these five points, beginning with an artifact of mass production and the assembly line that makes history tangible.

The Waters–Genter Company introduced the Toastmaster in 1926, based on the invention by Charles Strite of Stillwater, Minnesota, and billed it as the world's first automatic, pop-up toaster. It retailed for a hefty $12.50 and sold well, working with a system of clock-like timer, springs, and switches and sporting a gleaming, nickel-plated, art deco design.[9] Unlike a modern toaster, the machine is heavy, weighing four-and-a-half pounds. It is a streamlined, impressive artifact of industrial technology and consumer appreciation. The distinct ticking it produces while toasting bread does not fail to impress the observer with its reliability (and its sturdiness means that it is still possible to demonstrate its operation), while its six side air vents connote speedy efficiency.

Memory of the toaster as an innovation and a money-maker remains vibrant. A modern business whose name recognizes its origins, the Toastmaster Corporation issued a press release early in 1997 entitled "Toastmaster Introduces Chromatics Line of Chrome Appliances." In it, a company spokesman cites a story appearing in *The Wall Street Journal* that suggests why the chrome look continues to appeal to consumers: "[D]ifferent people like it for different reasons, some see it as clean and high-tech, while others view it as old-fashioned and industrial."[10]

What a centerpiece the Toastmaster becomes for multiple lines of historical inquiry: industrial technology, modernist design, consumerism and the expansion of a mass culture, urban growth and the ways its electrification and automation affected the status of women. In one sense, the Toastmaster acts as a symbol for an age, and hence as an abstraction that cannot capture an era's complexity; but it also helps to make the past tangible and therefore more easily grasped by students sitting in a sterile classroom. It is fun to look at and to touch and allows students to wonder how a machine could represent a significant change in one's life. (And, lest anyone conclude that such machines are unalloyed joys, students need only to consider the implications of spending limited financial resources in order to have them.)

What about the era that does not have its Toastmaster? First, a little imagination quickly suggests many possible equivalents: arrowhead, scarab, coin, illuminated page, woven carpet, stamp—all are reminders that the human condition is a material one and that one entryway into the past is through the simplicity of a single object thoughtfully considered. Second, the object is a means, not an end, for perceiving how material culture embodies the ideas, beliefs, fears, and hopes held by a people living in a specific time and place, and helps us see how they both were affected by those things and acted upon them. As such, the object may be present in the classroom only through illustration. It should remain, even so, eductive. The fact that the bowls of English-made clay tobacco pipes grew larger during the seventeenth and eighteenth centuries as tobacco became more affordable is useful knowledge not only to the archaeologist who depends upon such artifacts to help date a site, but also to the student seeking a way to enter a world based to a nearly unimaginable degree on the production of a single staple, in an environment increasingly dependent upon slave labor—a world that may not be so easily accessible relying only on the documentary record.[11]

Few periods in American history have captured the imagination with stories of individuals and communities to the extent that the Civil War has. In his annual message to Congress in 1862, Abraham Lincoln noted that, "*We* cannot escape history. . . . No personal significance, or insignificance, can spare one or another of us. The fiery trial through which we pass will light us down, in honor or dishonor, to the latest generation."[12] Lincoln understood history in personal terms, as something shaped by people and their actions. Similarly, what made Ken Burns' documentary *The Civil War* memorable is that he succeeded in telling the war's stories through the lives and words of those who lived them. So effective was Burns' accomplishment that Major Sullivan Ballou's 1861 letter to his wife, written just before his death at the first battle of Bull Run and poignantly capturing how entwined personal loss and a sense of honor could be, features prominently in both the film's accompanying book and soundtrack.[13]

It is a story both monumental—literally and metaphorically—and personal, rending a highly literate society that documented an almost countless number of accounts of its travail in letters, diaries, newspapers, and books. For us, these accounts not only provide a richness of sources from which we can ask, with Homer, "What god drove them to fight with such a fury?" They also help to keep the struggle understandable as a human contest. Questions of why the North won, why the South lost, who freed the slaves, or what it was like for the soldiers remain topics in which, even in the maelstrom of war, the human element remains paramount.

Human action is inextricably bound with storytelling. To narrate, etymologically speaking, is to *know*. Story resists quantification, and as we rob the past of its tangibleness and its personhood, we also lose the ability to tell stories that explain it. We gain understanding through storytelling—the words "story" and "history" share a root meaning of "inquiry." Ancient peoples, of course, knew this linkage. Stories are at the heart of biblical literature and ancient mythologies, both of which share a faith in storytelling's ability to do more than amuse, but to explain the past, account for the present, and suggest a direction of the future.

Thucydides cautioned that there would be readers of his history of the Peloponnesian War who would be disappointed by the absence of romance; "but if it be judged useful," he concluded, "by those inquirers who desire an exact knowledge of the past as an aid to the understanding of the future, which in the course of human beings must resemble if it does not reflect it, I shall be content."[14] What makes his work "a possession for all time," however, owes less to his attempt at accuracy and faithfulness to his sources than to his ability to relate with an inexorable narrative line his account of what he took to be "the greatest movement yet known to history."[15]

Thucydides' example continues to be a worthy one for teachers of history. The elements of good narration—people responding uniquely to external events, decisions that could have been made differently, action without the benefit of complete knowledge—are evident in other parts of the past, just as they are in the present. Telling stories to students, unfortunately, has been misconstrued as reducing the teacher's status to one of entertainer. However, at least one notable historian, Gerda Lerner, has justified this role:

> There is nothing shabby about this performance aspect of the teacher's skill, this trick of the magician and the artist. When we succeed in our performance role as teachers, we extend the learner's thoughts and feelings, so that he can move into past worlds and share the thoughts and values of another place and time.[16]

The long-standing popularity of television soap operas attests to our desire to enter others' lives. Confusing purpose with content is no excuse for shying away from narration's power, although as teachers we might be required to give up some of our worksheets in favor of stories we know thoroughly and believe retain the ability to explain.

In understanding the ever-changing present, however, we must take cognizance of the fact that our history needs to remain fluid if it is to retain the power to explain. During the years of the Reagan presidency, I devoted a considerable part of a survey course in United States history to the Cold War, especially as it related to the threat of nuclear warfare. When I began my teaching career, the school where I taught was old enough to have retained a basement that had been designated as a civil defense shelter and which was still equipped with cases of distilled water and canned food. Not long afterward, the supplies were removed—rats, leakage, and asbestos had become problems—but I retained a cardboard drum with its supplies—the SK IV Sanitation Kit, dated 1965—that was designed to serve as a portable toilet. It was a remarkably evocative artifact about a past that was not remote enough for comfort. This was a time, after all, when the school board still thought it was necessary to issue a policy statement detailing how early dismissal and the bus routes would be managed in the event of an imminent nuclear exchange. Never did I unpack the kit before students without them responding with appropriately ribald observations about their likely physical state in the event of such an emergency.

In a day when we were being told that with enough shovels we could survive a nuclear holocaust, it was natural to want to know just how a nuclear weapon worked, what would happen if one were detonated over a city, and if, indeed, a nuclear attack would be survivable in any meaningful sense. Ours was not the first generation of children to face so gloomy a prospect, as was demonstrated in *The Atomic Cafe* (1982), the documentary quilt of federal films on nuclear war preparedness produced by Jayne Loader, Kevin Rafferty, and Pierce Rafferty. What was different was the amount of information and debate about nuclear war that was present in the 1980s. It was an easy thing to discuss with the class what people thought about the atomic bomb when it was first used in 1945, or how they reacted to hydrogen bomb testing in the following decade, or the degree of seriousness with which they responded to the showdown over Cuba in 1962. The history I was teaching was informed by the concerns (and not, I hasten to add, the polemics) of the present, so much so that as I look back upon that time now, in a time after the demise of the Soviet Union, it appears very strange and remote. Teaching about the era from today's vantage might require examining the same events, but from a different perspective in which destruction by nuclear weapons appears less likely than the unleashing of anthrax, and the term "superpower" appears less frequently than "rogue state." (The glibness with which the testing of atomic weapons in India and Pakistan—nations sharing a common border—is compared to the situation between international powers like the United States and the Soviet Union also acts as a reminder that whatever lessons history might teach are best accompanied with reminders of the limitations of analogical thinking.)

One of the most frightening aspects of the Cold War was the worry that political leaders were losing their capacity to choose freely between peaceful and horrifyingly destructive courses of action. "For history," observed R. G. Collingwood, "the object to be discovered is not the mere event, but the thought expressed in it."[17] Collingwood was asserting that historians do not inquire into causes in the expectation of revealing a contingency that renders human agency null. For Collingwood, "The cause of the event . . . means the thought in the mind of the person by whose agency the event came about: and this is not something other than the event, it is inside of the event itself."[18]

I know of no topic more difficult to teach in high school than the American practice of slavery. White and black students alike come to this topic with attitudes largely fixed by years of close, yet paradoxically distant, proximity to one another. While white students often want to view slavery as an issue that has been addressed and is no longer a relevant concern, black students are frequently suspicious that the attitudes which made its horrors real continue to lie not far below the surface of public civility. I have often begun the study of slavery with a small collection of historical documents: wills that mention the disposal of slaves, a book of laws containing statutes enacted after the Nat Turner uprising of 1831, and a few scraps of paper which once served as errand notes for slaves dispatched to a store. Students are usually most interested in the notes. In them, slavery appears not as an impersonal economic institution, but as a human one in which people were required to interact regularly with other people they knew. The students ask what prevented masters from entrusting their slaves with oral messages—the presumption of a slave's forgetfulness, knowledge of a merchant's suspiciousness, or recognition that written permission was required to leave a plantation? When they read a message like, "lete cela hav too pears of scus" students cannot help but wonder aloud what the storekeeper thought when he first unfolded the paper: was the owner nearly as illiterate as the slave? were things somehow unjust? Or was the old person who wrote the note getting along in years?[19]

Seen in these terms, slavery becomes an institution built upon countless human decisions lacking inevitability and imbued instead with choice—about indentured servitude increasingly distinguishing between black and white laborers, about the divided mind of a slaveholder and apostle of liberty like Thomas Jefferson, about the toughening of laws regulating slave behavior after the Turner uprising, about the subtle and various forms of resistance by enslaved people determined to survive and even sustain a distinctive culture. Concomitant with the telling of stories like these is the trust required of the teacher who must lead a class to participate in stories that are often laden with pain. In this postmodernist age that is as facile at deconstructing meaning as it is impotent to discover it, at a time when it is fashionable to doubt any narrative's ability to draw us together, in a culture that is fearfully insistent on distinguishing our differences in a desperate search for identity, the teacher discovers the greatest obstacles to the teaching of history.

This book's remaining chapters offer the only way this teacher has known of negotiating these obstacles in an attempt to make the past relevant through the creation of histories that speak to the present. They are rooted in a personal understanding and acceptance, the result of years of struggle and growth, of who I am as a teacher and what it means to *profess*—to openly affirm—the calling of teaching. To describe these chapters as model lessons is to characterize them wrongly, for they lack the detail of such plans and, most importantly, they reflect too much of who I am as a teacher to be offered, much less accepted, as patterns from which a series of lessons can be cut, with no regard for the teacher who must wear the clothes. So, in this sense they are autobiographical, but in their presentation there may be enough examples of coming to terms with the past to help others who in their own ways must confront this same challenge.

Notes

[1] Jo Anne Pagano, *Exiles and Communities: Teaching in the Patriarchal Wilderness* (Albany: State University of New York Press, 1990) xiv.

[2] Pagano 2.

[3] John Dewey, *Democracy and Education: An Introduction to the Philosophy of Education* (New York: The Macmillan Company, 1916) 251.

[4] Dewey 250–1.

[5] Pagano 85.

[6] Gerda Lerner, *Why History Matters: Life and Thought* (New York: Oxford University Press, 1997) 117.

[7] Deborah P. Britzman, *Practice Makes Perfect: A Critical Study of Learning* (Albany: State University of New York Press, 1991) 43.

[8] Pagano 86.

[9] This description draws on information taken from the Toastmaster Corporation's website. Toastmaster Incorporated. "Timeline of Toast." N. D. <http://www.toastmaster.com/about/timeline/more_1926.html> (27 December 1997). See also Michele Herman, "The Electronic Toaster," *American Heritage* 41 (December 1990): 36–7.

[10] Charles Williamson, editor. "Toastmaster Introduces Chromatics Line of Chrome Appliances," January 18, 1997, <http://www.toastmaster.com/press/chromatics.html> (27 December 1997).

[11] For an evocative recreation of a forgotten life utilizing fragments of a smoking pipe (and the reliance on the bore diameter of pipe stems as well as bowl size for dating an archaeological site) see James Deetz, *Flowerdew Hundred: The Archaeology of a Virginia Plantation, 1619–1864* (Charlottesville: University

Press of Virginia, 1993), especially Chapters 1 and 6.

[12] Abraham Lincoln, "Annual Message to Congress, December 1, 1862" in *Speeches and Writings, 1859–1865* (New York: Library of America, 1989) 415 (emphasis in original).

[13] Geoffrey C. Ward with Ric Burns and Ken Burns, *The Civil War: An Illustrated History* (New York: Alfred A. Knopf, 1990) 82–83 and *The Civil War: Original Soundtrack Recording*, Elektra Nonesuch 9–79256–2.

[14] Sobert B. Strassler, ed., *The Landmark Thucydides: A Comprehensive Guide to the Pelopponesian War* (New York: The Free Press, 1996) 16.

[15] Strassler 3.

[16] Lerner 127.

[17] R. G. Collingwood, *The Idea of History* (Oxford: University Press, 1946) 214.

[18] Collingwood 214–5.

[19] See the more detailed exposition and documentation of these notes in Chapter 3.

Chapter 6

Fridays Belong to Ned Cobb

"I'm comin to that, I just have to tell this first," is how Theodore Rosengarten recounts the Alabama farmer Ned Cobb (1885–1973) responding to his children's attempts to remind him of his story's direction.[1] Rosengarten was interviewing Cobb in 1969 about his participation in the Alabama Sharecroppers Union, a participation that led in December 1932 to Cobb's confrontation with deputy sheriffs—who were trying to confiscate a neighbor's livestock—their exchange of gunfire, and his subsequent, lengthy prison term. Quickly realizing that Cobb was a born storyteller, Rosengarten returned during the next few years in order to record this man's account of his life and times. Rosengarten soon abandoned a long list of questions he had prepared and began instead to give free rein to the old man's remarkable memory—one that allowed him to people his stories with the names of over four hundred individuals. What emerged was the life history of a man who, to paraphrase William Faulkner (whose Snopes family paralleled Cobb's on the other side of the color line), not merely endured, but prevailed.

Ned Cobb's life was a long one: "I can't reach the hill like I used to could but I'm not at a standstill yet," he concluded in his eighty-fifth year when he had finally sold his mule (he never owned a tractor) and declined to raise a crop of cotton. Cobb was of that first generation born after slavery's demise, and, although he lived a long life in a time of great change, he never escaped a sense of the past in which slavery loomed large. His father had spent the first fifteen years of his life in slavery, which Cobb thought had marked his behavior for the rest of his days. "My daddy was a free man but in his acts he was a slave. Didn't look ahead to profit hisself in nothin that he done. Is it or not a old slave act? Anything a man do in a slum way and don't care way, I just lap it right back on slavery time days."[2]

After spending a dozen years in prison, Cobb returned home to children who had come of age maintaining the family in the absence of their father, a wife who was in declining health, and a landscape that was both strange and familiar. He was a mule farmer in a place now dominated by tractors, and a tenant who now had to learn about federal farm programs, but he remained a black man in a place that continued to require black men, especially those with ambition who had to "be ready to defend [themselves] against words and bullets, bullets and words." Looking back across his life as he neared the end of it, Cobb allowed that he felt "a certain loyalty to the state of Alabama: I was born and raised here and I have sowed my labor into the earth and lived to reap only a part of it, not all that was mine by human right."[3]

Throughout a life that began in 1885 and remained active until his death at age eighty-eight, Ned Cobb's history personalized important themes in the nation's struggle to define the relationship between black and white Americans. Even more importantly, Cobb's life shines light on those elusive qualities that humans have always sought to understand and without which, William Faulkner concluded, "any story is ephemeral and doomed—love and honor and pity and pride and compassion and sacrifice."[4] Illuminating both American history and human existence, Ned Cobb is worth listening to, especially in the classroom.

Fridays, therefore, belonged to Ned Cobb. An experienced teacher senses the rhythm of work that exists in a school's calendar and, despite a closed door, how it permeates the classroom. Co-opting this rhythm for one's own purposes can save a measure of frustration when one has a room full of students ready for the weekend and who are unwilling to do much class work on a Friday, for it allows for something more substantial than might otherwise be expected. Even though my students made for a somewhat skeptical adolescent audience, on Fridays they came to expect, even demand, that I read aloud an excerpt from the transcription that Theodore Rosengarten had made from his hours of interviews with Ned Cobb: *All God's Dangers*.

Finding selections to read was never difficult, although limiting their number was. While Cobb's rural life was alien to my students, his experiences were often appreciated. Consider this selection of topics, which I marked for reading, as arresting entry points into incidents that characterized his life:

> The Bible says. 'What has been will be again.' And Grandma Cealy said a right smart about this: that that day was comin. Colored people once knowed what it was like to live under freedom before they got over in this country, and they would know it again.
>
> I was nine years old when my mother died; I was too little to re-

> member the date of the month but she died in August and I just lackin from the date she died up until the twenty-eighth day of December of bein nine years old. If I had a twenty-dollar bill this mornin for every time I seed my daddy beat up my mother and beat up my stepmother I wouldn't be settin here this morning because I'd have up in the hundreds of dollars.
>
> First time my daddy hired me out—he never did hire me out but twice; he kept me right under his thumb until the year I was nineteen years old. 1904, he hired me out. He'd kept me around him all the time until then but he thought he could help hisself more by drawin on me.
>
> 1905, I was beginnin to pick up and spur my own horse then. One Sunday in October—I disremember whether it was the first Sunday, second Sunday, third Sunday, or the fourth Sunday, but it was October—I heard that this girl—I done waited as long as I could. I loved her, I loved her.[5]

Notice that this brief selection of passages follows Cobb's life only up to the time of his first and long-lasting marriage, twenty years of a life that spanned over eight decades!

No sooner would one of my classes study the Reconstruction era (before the end of the first semester) than we would begin reading selections from *All God's Dangers*. Ned Cobb would be a companion for the remainder of the school year. By then, the room would be festooned with sheets of paper chronologically connecting Cobb's memories to the kinds of things that were part of the official curriculum. Cobb was young enough to have seen his daddy "stripped of everything he had" by white landowners in the year that Booker T. Washington was invited by Theodore Roosevelt to a White House luncheon, provoking enough controversy that the President did not repeat such an invitation again. As a young man, Cobb visited Tuskegee where he heard Washington speak on the "celebration days" of commencement. Years later, he believed that he would not "boost Booker Washington today up to everything that was industrious and right" because Washington, Cobb concluded, "didn't feel for and didn't respect his race of people enough to go rock bottom with em. He leaned too much to the white people that controlled the money."[6] Cobb helped to make Washington a living, controversial leader again, instead of the patron saint of self-improvement he has been portrayed as, while also rendering his own coming of age in an environment designed to insure his subordination.

Which aspect of Ned Cobb was most important? Was it that part of him involved in the early days of the Depression in a labor movement that was ominously (and, for Cobb, cryptically) described as a "soviet" union, or the man who struggled to come to terms with his father while being a parent absent from his nine children for a dozen years? Cobb, the man of a particular time and place; or Cobb, the man wrestling with issues common to humanity? Rosengarten explained how he understood what Cobb had done by listening to his story:

> The framing [of this account] says that beyond 'tractable' issues such as social justice, remain 'intractable' issues which are the real ground of our human estate. That timeless, even cyclical, frame was repeated in Nate's life-work: he began a sharecropper under his daddy and he ended a sharecropper under his son. He quotes the Biblical phrase—Once a man, twice a child—which, when recognized by the extended family at large, is a great source of strength for the individual, because people in his family and in his region do grow old with grace.[7]

Ultimately, I think the students sensed that these two sides of Cobb were too intertwined to be separated. My suspicion, however, is that the latter aspect of the man—the one who wrestled with intractable issues—made farmer Cobb someone the students wanted to know.

Ned Cobb's identity was bound up with struggles that were uniquely his in a particular time and place. His stories, however, do more than inform; they also provide a critical insight into American society, especially given Cobb's ability to extract meaning from his narrative. In analyzing "the longing for critical voice" felt by those whose narratives have been denied hearing, bell hooks has observed: "Part of our struggle for radical black subjectivity is the quest to find ways to construct self and identity that are oppositional and liberatory."[8] Our greatest lesson in studying Ned Cobb comes from looking at the way he constructed an identity that survived in a hostile environment, yet remained in opposition to the values that society attempted to impose. Cobb constantly sought ways to assert his liberty, whether it meant being as economically self-sufficient as possible, refusing repeated offers of parole if he renounced his union involvement, or expressing wonderment that his family "was just scared to death and ashamed" of his membership in a union organization that had brought him such grief.[9]

Listening to an individual's story is only one way of fashioning an understanding of the past—in fact, what one person can know is hedged by the limitations of our judgments and the incompleteness of our experiences. An era's literary fiction is also illuminating when it attempts to portray the past in light of its own "present" attitudes. The historian Richard N. Current has observed that "novelists may have a much greater influence than historians do on popular conceptions of the past." Current makes a useful distinction between *historical fiction*, which "presents imaginary characters and events against a background of presumed historical facts," and *fictional history*, which "pretends to deal with real persons and events but actually reshapes them—and thus rewrites the past." For Current, writers of the latter are more troubling: "Past reality and present fantasy blend more and more into an inseparable mix."[10]

As a teacher of history, I find the works of the former more intriguing. Two novels in particular, by offering sharply different views of the era of Reconstruction and the bane of racism, provide a background for understanding the life of someone like Ned Cobb. Both novels are valuable for they portray the attitudes of the period in which they were written, probably with greater accuracy than the era in which their characters are set (although for the first novel the two periods are nearly the same).

The author of the first novel was a transplanted northerner who tried to resettle in the post–Civil War South. Albion Winegar Tourgée (1838–1905) was in a jubilant mood on 10 January 1879, when he wrote from Greensboro, North Carolina to his wife, Emma. Despite complaints of neuralgia, crippling headaches, paralysis in his right hand, and the strain of seeing through only one eye, he had pushed himself to finish a legal work undertaken with the help of his friend and neighbor, Stephen A. Douglas, Jr. Now, the manuscript for *A Digest of Cited Cases in the North Carolina Reports*—described by Tourgée as his "magnum opus"—was finished. "Today at 7:22 p.m. we wrote the last case! Already, I begin to feel tired and almost lost." Little wonder that he felt "almost lost." Tourgée had accumulated several painful reputations since journeying to North Carolina at the close of the Civil War: as the superior court judge frustrated in his attempts to prosecute members of the Ku Klux Klan; as the businessman whose tool-handle manufactory failed during the 1873 depression; as the politician repeatedly thwarted in his bids for elected office; and, perhaps most hurtful to his family, as the carpetbagger shunned by genteel society. Now, ironically, Albion Tourgée had to communicate his good news to Emma by mail, because since the previous autumn she had resided in Erie, Pennsylvania, preferring separation from her husband to living any longer in the South, which she had come to despise.[11]

Had Albion Tourgée reflected on the struggling years he believed benevolently spent trying to remake the South, he might have recalled the angry words he penned in 1877: "Everyone who has fought for the country's integrity or favored the policy of reconstruction will have reason to curse the day he did so."[12] Having experienced more frustration and penury than even someone as cantankerous as he could endure, Tourgée was now ready to take his wife to the promises offered in Denver or the opportunities beckoning from New York City. He knew that whatever prospects he faced, however, North Carolina, and the South in general, would continue to haunt him. With perhaps only a dim awareness of where his pastime would lead him, Tourgée embarked on a writing career that would dramatize his belief in the foolishness of the nation's halfhearted attempt to reconstruct a culture as distinct and defiant as the South's. The publishing firm of Fords, Howard, and Hulbert had assured Tourgée that, rather than reprint anew his 1874 novel, *Toinette*—a tale of the relationship between a one-time slave, a nearly white woman named Toinette, and her exploitative yet loving former master—the publishers preferred that he get a new manuscript into shape as soon as possible based on his experiences in North Carolina, soon to be entitled by Tourgée *A Fool's Errand*. "You doubtless have much that you would like to ventilate," wrote J. R. Howard, who closed his admonitory letter "with congratulation at your new damnation of Yankeeism."[13] In his passionate recounting of a time in his life that seemed to have marked him more profoundly than his experience as a wounded Union army officer, Tourgée would reap fame, controversy, and wealth beyond any he had dreamed of.

Once begun, Tourgée poured out over almost thirty years a torrent of novels, stories, articles, editorials, essays, and even the plaintiff's brief in the landmark Supreme Court case of *Plessy v. Ferguson*. His breadth of interests was most often wed to his passion for social justice, hence his commitment in the 1890s to an increasingly eviscerated civil rights movement. The work that brought him the most immediate and longest-lasting acclaim, however, was the one most autobiographical of his carpetbagger experience: *A Fool's Errand, By One of the Fools,* published in 1879.

Tourgée's faith in the Civil War's remedial effects centered on a conviction he was disabused of by the years he spent in North Carolina (during which he had hoped to recuperate from war wounds, take advantage of new business opportunities, and put into practice his training as a lawyer) that proper education would allow white southerners to break through the strictures imposed by their closed society and enable black southerners to assume the responsibilities of citizenship.[14] The federal government's retreat from Reconstruction in the 1870s taught Tourgée additional, more complicated lessons. Black southerners, having to adjust to the realities of the postwar South rather than the promises fostered by emancipation and enfranchisement, would have to live dependent upon the generosity of enlightened former masters while learning habits of industry—a not very promising prospect. Continuing to cling to the image of a Cavalier aristocracy, white southerners were failing to understand that new economic and social conditions brought opportunities that had been denied to the South when slavery shut off the region from developments in the rest of the nation. Most telling about Tourgée's thinking was the realization that northerners had believed foolishly that the Appomattox surrender represented white southerners' acknowledgment of mistaken convictions. Northern refusal to heed warnings that the peace was being lost, as southerners worked to rebuild their society along familiar patterns of white supremacy, provided Tourgée with the vigor that infused his best writings.[15]

Late in his life, when his message was already being forgotten, Albion Tourgée remembered how the idea of *A Fool's Errand* had come to him: "After a sleepless night spent in restless review of events which had occurred since the close of the war of Rebellion, especially in regard to the relations of Northern and Southern ideas," Tourgée recounted, "I wakened my wife and said: 'I am going to write a book and call it *A Fool's Errand.*'" Immediately rising, Tourgée went to another room of his Raleigh, North Carolina residence, where he was then working as a federal pension agent, and proceeded to write four chapters. Little could he have foreseen, on that Sunday morning in July 1877, the reception that awaited the novel's publication two years later. In January 1880, Tourgée's father, Valentine Tourgée, wrote to him about events in the family's hometown of Kingsville, Ohio. A bookseller had been unable to keep on hand a supply of the just-released novel; the publisher had told the dealer that the firm had been between 1,200 and 1,500 copies behind on orders for some time; and a friend reported seeing six copies of the book sold while waiting for his train at a nearby station. Meanwhile, a Republican office holder in New Orleans was complaining to the publishers that *A Fool's Errand* "is not for sale at the bookstores, and southern sentiment is such, that I doubt if the dealers care to make any effort to sell the work." Although published anonymously, Tourgée would soon be known, both derisively and affectionately, as "the Fool," the epithet he had given to the novel's carpetbagger protagonist.[16]

The author of *A Fool's Errand* dedicated his work "to the ancient and honorable family of Fools" of which he was a member. For this "One of the Fools," the difference between himself and Noah, another relation, was that, after earnestly making all worthwhile preparations, the waters prevailed against the Fool while the Wise Men laughed. For Colonel Comfort Servosse, the novel's northern hero hoping to find economic opportunity and a healthful climate in the South, the name of "Fool" was synonymous with the contemptuous label of "Carpetbagger." In the North, Tourgée had been given to understand that a carpetbagger was "a man without means, character, or occupation; an adventurer, a camp-follower, a 'bummer.'" Such a simple, if unsavory, definition failed, however, to capture the depth of feeling involved when southerners used the epithet. For them, a carpetbagger was much more: "a man of Northern birth + an abolitionist (according to the Southern definition) + an incarnation of Northern hate, envy, spleen, greed, hypocrisy, and all uncleanness."[17] Scorned in the North, detested in the South, the carpetbagger's best intentions were but folly. Unable to recognize his foolishness, the carpetbagger was destined for destruction.

Tourgée quickly followed *A Fool's Errand* with the sequel, *Bricks Without Straw*, a novel which sympathetically portrays Reconstruction's effects upon the freedmen. In describing a raid against a freedmen's settlement perpetrated by the Ku Klux Klan, Tourgée assured his readers that his account added nothing to what had been documented by congressional investigations of Klan activity. For Tourgée, the incident itself was less important than the time's general climate of intimidation. "The facts are of no special interest, however, except as illustrations of the underlying spirit and cause of this strange epidemic of violence."[18]

It is against this background that I ask students to read a powerful excerpt from *A Fool's Errand*. By the winter of 1868, Colonel Comfort Servosse had unknowingly made himself an outlaw among the people of Verdenton, North Carolina, where he had hoped to establish himself at the abandoned plantation of Warrington. What Servosse had done was successfully campaign for election to a post desired by few native southerners: delegate to the state constitutional convention, charged with incorporating into fundamental charter the dictates of the Reconstruction Congress of the United States. It is at this point that Servosse's life dramatically intersects with those of the freedmen who live nearby. In the chapter "A New Institution," Servosse begins to realize the import of white hostility toward the perceived new order. Servosse had known of "an industrious and thrifty blacksmith" named Bob Martin who, although he lived in a distant part of the county, "was noted as one of the most independent and self-reliant of his people in all political as well as pecuniary matters."[19] Together with a small group of freedmen, Martin stood in front of the Fool one day in the winter of 1868, carefully peeling off his shirt to demonstrate to Servosse his regret that the Ku Kluxers were neither the ghostly figures nor prankster boys the ignorant and the foolish (like Servosse) had made them out to be. Martin's back, Servosse was horrified to realize, had just been furrowed by the whip of someone expert at disciplining field hands. The Klan had visited Martin the previous evening.

Martin explains to the Colonel what happened and with allowances for the literary taste of the day to render speech in dialect makes clear why he was so mistreated.[20]

> I know'd der was'n't a better blacksmif in de country, an' thought I hed things jes' ez good ez I wanted 'em. When ther come an election, I sed my say, did my own votin', an tole de other colored people dey waz free, an' hed a right ter du de same. Thet's bad doctrine up in our country. De white folks don't like ter hear it, and 'specially don't like ter hear a nigger say it. Dey don't mind 'bout our gittin' on ef dey hev a mortgage, so't de 'arnin's goes into ther pockets; nor 'bout our votin', so long ez we votes ez dey tells us. Dat's dare idea uv liberty fer a nigger.[21]

Servosse's education about conditions in the South as they really existed had just begun. Although organized terrorist activity against black Americans fluctuated in frequency across the next century, the underlying spirit of persecution did not. There is little in this statement that Ned Cobb could not appreciate or had not experienced himself.

When Servosse learns that Martin has also served in the Union army, he realizes a bond between them that reinforces his sympathy for a fellow human's plight:

> A man has a right to protect himself and his family; and, if our government is too blind or too weak to put down this new rebellion, there are only three courses before us,—you and me, and those who stood with us: the one is to fight the devil with fire,—to kill those who kill,—guard the fords, and, whenever we see a man in disguise, shoot him down; another is to give up every thing else for the privilege of living here; and the third is to get away.

As they leave each other's company, each man resolves to find a way to resist the evil that has descended upon them. And while, by the novel's end, a sense of resolution is reached, the "unsolved problem" of reconciling white and black remains for others to wrestle with.[22]

Albion Winegar Tourgée must have felt a forgotten man at the time of his death in 1905. The law of the land was that of Jim Crow, and it would be nearly fifty years before the opinion he had advanced in his brief for the Supreme Court case *Plessy v. Ferguson*—that segregation is unconstitutional "because it denies equal protection of the law to all classes of citizens; perpetuates inequalities in the enjoyment of their rights; perpetuates race prejudice and deprives citizens of liberty and immunity without due process of law"—was accepted as constitutional principle.[23] So far removed from the days of *A Fool's Errand* did Tourgée feel that he wrote to Theodore Roosevelt in 1901 (in a letter congratulating him for showing the forthrightness to meet with Booker T. Washington) confessing he no longer believed that the education of black southerners would engender racial harmony. "I realize now that . . . education does not eradicate prejudice, but intensifies it—Christianity does not condemn or prevent injustice done to the weak by the strong, but encourages and excuses it."[24] These are the words of a bitter man who had believed greatly and been mightily disillusioned.

Tourgée certainly had good reason for pointing to the weaknesses of both education and Christianity as forces that oppose racism. Already, he had witnessed the meteoric rise to fame of Thomas Dixon, a formally educated Baptist minister of blazing abilities, an individual with a passion—if not a distinguished talent—for writing, who possessed an obdurate conviction that black Americans could never be citizens because of their inherent inferiority.

Thomas Dixon, Jr. (1864–1946) was born near Shelby, North Carolina and grew up in a family familiar with both postwar poverty and politics—a favorite uncle was an important leader of the Ku Klux Klan in the western part of the state, while his father was a farmer, storekeeper, and preacher who struggled to keep his family respectable.[25] His father's faith in education sent his namesake first to Wake Forest College and then to Johns Hopkins University, where the young Dixon befriended Woodrow Wilson, then a graduate student. After dabbling in politics as a state legislator too young even to vote for himself, Dixon prospered as the restless pastor of several Baptist congregations, including the Twenty-Third Street Church in New York City, where his passionate sermons attracted the favorable attention of John D. Rockefeller.

Although a popular Chautauqua lecturer, Dixon sought a wider audience for a message he felt increasingly burdened to deliver, a message that the new century's generation of historians also were fashioning: that the years of Reconstruction had been a farcical tragedy for the South ending only when white southerners were able to restore order and sanity. Only a southerner with his background and passion could faithfully tell such a story, Dixon believed, and so he began to write a series of novels that were intended less as literature than as polemic. Perhaps more than any historian of his day, Dixon helped shape the popular view that portrayed the era of Reconstruction as a morality play peopled with heroic and noble white southern men; white southern women worth more than any earthly kingdom; scheming, vengeful, foolish white northerners (except for the martyred Lincoln); and, most hateful of all, black southern men who, once corrupted by the taste of liberty, reverted to their beastly nature.

"We are too close to realize the tragedy [of Reconstruction]," Dixon wrote in the last years of his long life. "The scholar and historian must have the perspective of more than a hundred years in which to tell this story to make it credible."[26] Unfortunately, Dixon was neither a scholar nor a historian, and he was willing to write long before a century had passed the most *in*credible stories about the era, stories that in their day proved far more popular than had those of Tourgée a generation earlier.

When Walter Hines Page agreed to publish a first novel written by his longtime acquaintance Thomas Dixon, he likely had no idea how successful the book would be, at least in terms of financially securing the fledging firm of Doubleday, Page and Company. Published in 1902, *The Leopard's Spots: A Romance of the White Man's Burden—1865–1900* sold very well and, although not reaching bestseller status, achieved a great notoriety.[27] Dixon even found himself defending his motivation for writing the novel to his brother Clarence: "You said what my bitterest critics who wrote with Prussic Acid never thought of—that my *purpose* was to make money. This is of course true, just as your purpose is to make money preaching—and I confess the fact, but I thought it rather brutal for you to *say* so."[28]

Even so, Dixon had found a theme with a ready audience, a theme he did little to change in the over twenty novels he wrote during the next three decades. In *The Leopard's Spots*, the Preacher asserts that "we have not only not settled this [Negro] question,—we haven't even faced the issues."[29] Of all the hopeless attempts to overcome the inequality between the races, declared the Preacher, none had been more forlorn than putting faith in education's redemptive power:

> 'Education! Can you change the colour of his skin, the kink of his hair, the bulge of his lips, the spread of his nose, or the beat of his heart, with a spelling book? The Negro is the human donkey. You can train him, but you can't make of him a horse. Mate him with a horse, you lose the horse, and get a larger donkey called a mule, incapable of preserving his species. What is called our race prejudice is simply God's first law of nature—the instinct of self-preservation.'[30]

Dixon was nothing if not consistent, even if it meant that his readers drifted away as times changed and he did not. In his last novel, written in the late 1930s, Dixon provided a contemporary setting to illustrate the threat of socialism, replacing Radical Republicans with equally manipulative Soviet communists intent on fomenting what Dixon's asserted was the black man's most outrageous hope: amalgamation with the white race. Dixon, however, remained adamant in his attitudes. Angela, the heroine in *The Flaming Sword*, contradicts Phil Stephens, who had "dreamed of a new South, about an uplifted prosperous people, black and white," after she returns from a lecture impressed with the words of Marcus Garvey. She challenges Phil, "Why not face the question squarely? We are playing with it. Our educational schemes are make-shifts. We could establish a colony of half a million Negroes in two years. They could lay the foundations of a Black Republic which would solve the problem on the only rational basis—friendly colonization."[31]

By the time he wrote his last novel, Dixon was living in an obscurity greater than any Tourgée had known. For both, fame had come early and faded during the remaining years of their lives. It was with *The Clansman: An Historical Romance of the Ku Klux Klan,* published in 1905, that Dixon gained a measure of immortality in his career as an author. This novel, inspiring first a play, then with parts of *The Leopard's Spots* finding an even wider audience through the new medium of the motion picture in D. W. Griffith's *The Birth of a Nation* (1915), attracted even the favorable comment of President Woodrow Wilson.[32] W. E. B. Du Bois captured both the film's essence and the reason it was so controversial in stating that "there was fed to the youth of the nation and to the unthinking masses as well as to the world a story which twisted the emancipation and enfranchisement of the slave in a great effort toward universal democracy, into an orgy of theft and degradation and wide rape of white women." Du Bois concluded that, because of the film, "The number of mob murders so increased that nearly one hundred Negroes were lynched during 1915 and a score of whites, a larger number than had occurred for more than a decade."[33]

The Clansman forms the second in a trilogy of novels treating what Dixon termed the "Race Conflict" in the South. Beginning with *The Leopard's Spots,* which traced the enfranchisement and disfranchisement of African-American citizens, the series included *The Clansman* and ended with *The Traitor* (1907), which described the disbanding of the Ku Klux Klan in the 1870s. "I have sought to preserve in this romance both the letter and the spirit of this remarkable period," Dixon says at the beginning of *The Clansman,* a "drama of fierce revenge" conducted by corrupt northern leaders under the leadership of congressman Thaddeus Stevens who sought "to Africanise ten great states of the American Union."[34] So great are Dixon's exaggerations and distortions of Reconstruction's failings, so heedless is he of the era's accomplishments, and so grotesquely does he portray the freedmen while glorifying white leadership, that it is difficult to read his work as anything other than an account of his own and of his time's prejudices. Not surprisingly, the novel was dedicated to Dixon's uncle, Leroy McAfee, "A Scotch-Irish Leader of the South" and a "Grand Titan of the Invisible Empire Ku Klux Klan."

It is from *The Clansman* that I share with students a difficult reading assignment, one that I do not assign without having first carefully prepared them for the racist attitudes they will confront. The story contrasts itself with the one told by Tourgée's Bob Martin about the mission of the Klan. Drawing on the cruelest of stereotypes, the novel's Marion Lenoir is raped in the presence of her mother by four Federal soldiers—"black janizaries"—led by Gus, a former slave of Piedmont's Cameron family and now an insufferable captain in the occupation army. Marion and her mother respond in the only noble way known to southern women so violated—they hurl themselves off nearby Lover's Leap. Missed the next morning by Ben Cameron, one of the novel's young protagonists (and presently to be revealed as the "Grand Dragon of the Realm"), the bodies are soon found, confirming Cameron's fears that had been aroused by his earlier discovery of barefoot tracks outside a window of the Lenoir home, prints characterized by "the enormous heel project[ing] backward, and in the hollow of the instep where dirt would scarcely be touched by an Aryan was the deep wide mark of the African's flat foot."[35]

Now Ben's father brings his medical and scientific knowledge to bear. Using a powerful microscope, Dr. Cameron replicates an experiment successfully conducted in Europe by examining the victims' retinas for an impression of the image made by their unspeakable experience. It is the mother's eye that preserved the sight, as Dr. Cameron describes it to Ben. "The bestial figure of a negro—his huge black hand plainly defined—the upper part of the face is dim, as if obscured by a gray mist of dawn—but the massive jaws and lips are clear—merciful God!—yes!—it's Gus!" Gus's sudden departure from Piedmont to the state capital at Columbia attested to his guilt; he was seized off the train and brought before the assemblage of the "silent horses and men with their tall spiked caps" which "made a picture such as the world had not seen since the Knights of the Middle Ages rode on their Holy Crusades."[36]

Against this backdrop students read the chapter "The Fiery Cross" for its description of the Klan's behavior, which is couched in terms of Christian righteousness; guardianship of the weak, orphaned, and widowed; defence of the Constitution; and execution of all constitutional laws. "Have mercy on the poor, the weak, the innocent and defenseless, and deliver us from the body of the Black Death," prays the Reverend Hugh McAlpin. "In a land of light and beauty and love our women are prisoners of danger and fear." Horrified to hear Dr. Cameron's charge against Gus, the clansmen are moved to tears and outrage when they hear Gus condemn himself via another of the doctor's talents: hypnotism. Once hypnotized, Gus reenacts the moment he approached his victim:

> He still wore his full Captain's uniform, its heavy epaulets flashing their gold in the unearthly light, his beastly jaws half covering the gold braid on the collar. His thick lips were drawn upward in an ugly leer and his sinister bead-eyes gleamed like a gorilla's. A single fierce leap and the black claws clutched the air slowly as if sinking into the soft white throat.

The clansmen are restrained from killing Gus on the spot only by Cameron's urging that they prepare an execution that will be recognized by fellow clansmen across the region, with Gus's body eventually dumped on the lawn of the lieutenant-governor's home in the state capital.[37]

It is a chilling story, not for the tale it relates, but for the truth it was taken to contain. Grotesque as the novel is and, fortunately, as obscure as it is today, its sentiments can still be heard to echo in the present whenever one hears sexuality associated with color, or humans with animals. It is a painful exercise to ask students to read the excerpt from *The Clansman*, although the novel's age and seeming remoteness from today make it easier to introduce the topic of prejudice and its underlying fear and hatred—a topic that is often avoided in the desire not to add to the difficulties of teaching by introducing anything discordant.

Having students reflect on Ned Cobb, Albion Tourgée, and Thomas Dixon as historical sources also reveals important distinctions between the three narratives. Although transmitted to us by another party, Cobb's remains a first-person account which gives us an individual who may not have understood, for example, the international connections of the union in which he was involved, but who was clear and articulate about the meaning of his own life. The stories Cobb was most practiced in telling compare with the thinly veiled autobiographical account of Albion Tourgée's experiences as a North Carolina carpetbagger in the generation before Cobb's birth. When it comes to Tourgée's relating of Bob Martin's encounter with the Klan, however, the author is much more clearly an observer recounting what he witnessed, and this only indirectly a participant. It is as if the voice has shifted from first- to second-person, while with Dixon, the voice shifts again, this time to the third-person. Lacking personal knowledge of the events he describes, except for those which may have come to him through his family, Dixon can only offer his impression of an impression relayed to him as explanation for the family's struggles. The differences leave us with Cobb's sharing of his personhood, Tourgée's plea on behalf of those with whom he knew and sympathized, and Dixon's apologia for the actions of a previous generation. The point here is not to depict one perspective as superior to another, but to illustrate how identity is fashioned from a variety of perspectives, some of which we may value for speaking the truth as we understand it more than others, but all of which are revealing.

While students quickly react to Ned Cobb, Albion Tourgée, and Thomas Dixon in fairly predictable ways, they respond more thoughtfully if the readings of these individuals are accompanied by opportunities to consider how identity is shaped by experience, how we understand our experiences, and the ways in which we generalize about the experiences of others. Whether they attempt to describe an experience that has affected them, or relate something they know about someone else, or describe those who they know not, students can be helped to understand how identity is made on both personal and historical levels. I have followed readings from *All God's Dangers* with a writing assignment asking students to relate an incident they believe they will one day tell their children, and to record a similar kind of experience told to them by someone who may not be alive to know their children. With *A Fool's Errand* and *The Clansman*, we have compared fiction to history in order to discern what we can believe and in what ways we can distinguish viewpoints that are honest but limited in knowledge from those that mix the same limitation with dishonesty. Perhaps these concerns are secondary to the ones measured by end-of-course examinations, which tend to ask jejune questions. Without at least attempting to raise such concerns, however, we leave our students unable to understand the connections between history and identity. "He had already figured out what was significant about his life," Theodore Rosengarten said of Ned Cobb, "or, more specifically, what stories raised the significant issues of the time we would want to know, as historians."[38] Surely this sentiment, applied to students as individuals and as members of a society bound by place and time, provides us with a touchstone for teaching history.

Notes

[1] Theodore Rosengarten, *All God's Dangers: The Life of Nate Shaw* (New York: Alfred A. Knopf, 1974) xv. Albert E. Stone thought that Rosengarten's use of aliases was unnecessary and testified "not only to Rosengarten's urge toward the mythic and fictional elements in the story and life he has recorded but also to a proprietary impulse which smacks of exploitation." Stone pointed out that Ned Cobb "was apparently pretty widely known in Alabama" and that his 1932 defiance of the inequities of the sharecropping system had been remembered in John Beecher's poem, "In Egypt Land, A Narrative Poem, 1940." In the paperback edition of *All God's Dangers*, Rosengarten revealed Cobb's identity and quoted from the poem. See Alfred E. Stone, *Autobiographical Occasions and Original Acts: Versions of American Identity from Henry Adams to Nate Shaw* (Philadelphia: University of Pennsylvania Press, 1982) 243.

[2] Rosengarten 26–7, 534.

[3] Rosengarten 452, 500.

[4] William Faulkner, "Nobel Prize Award Speech," Stockholm, Sweden, 10 December 1950, in Willard Thorp, *A Southern Reader* (New York: Alfred A. Knopf, 1955) 760.

[5] Rosengarten 7, 10, 37, 63.

[6] Rosengarten 542-3.

[7] George Abbott White, "The Hem of My Garment: An Interview with Theodore Rosengarten about the Makings of 'Nate Shaw,'" in *The Massachusetts Review* XXI (Winter 1980) 787–8.

[8] bell hooks, "Postmodern Blackness" in Walter Truett Anderson, ed., *The Truth About the Truth: De-Confusing and Re-Constructing the Postmodern World* (New York: G. P. Putnam's Sons, 1995) 121–2.

[9] Rosengarten 547.

[10] Richard Nelson Current, *Arguing with Historians: Essays on the Historical and the Unhistorical* (Middletown, Connecticut: Wesleyan University Press, 1987) 147–8, 161.

[11] Tourgée to Emma Tourgée, 10 January 1879, Albion W. Tourgée Papers, Chautauqua County Historical Society, Westfield, New York, microfilm, University of North Carolina at Greensboro; Richard N. Current, *Those Terrible Carpetbaggers: A Reinterpretation* (New York: Oxford University Press, 1988) 372–3.

[12] Tourgée to Dr. Southerland, 5 April 1877, Tourgée Papers.

[13] Fords, Howard, and Hulbert to Tourgée, 20 April 1877, Tourgée Papers.

[14] Tourgée offers an overview of his evolving attitudes towards the South and Reconstruction in his treatise, *An Appeal to Caesar* (New York: Fords, Howard, and Hulbert, 1884) 55–67.

[15] Tourgée's chief biographer is Otto H. Olsen, *Carpetbagger's Crusade: The Life of Albion Winegar Tourgée* (Baltimore: Johns Hopkins Press, 1965).

[16] Tourgée to James Carlton Young, 24 August 1903; Valentine Tourgée to his "Dear Children," 4 January 1880; C. W. Boothby to Fords, Howard, and Hulbert, January 22, 1879, Tourgée Papers.

[17] Albion W. Tourgée, *A Fool's Errand, By One of the Fools* (New York: Fords, Howard, and Hulbert, 1879) 4, 159, 161. According to Tourgée, southerners defined an abolitionist as "one who favors emancipation + infidel + all hell's accumulated horrors, 'not otherwise appropriated.'" Tourgée, *A Fool's Errand* 159.

[18] Albion W. Tourgée, *Bricks Without Straw: A Novel* (New York: Fords, Howard, and Hulbert, 1880) 289. Tourgée's concern that the greater truth of conditions in the South not be lost in the debate over lesser ones explains his desire to publish so soon after *A Fool's Errand* an expanded edition of the novel that included his factual supplement drawn from the thirteen volumes of testimony contained in the 1872 Report of the Joint Congressional Committee on the Ku-Klux Conspiracy. See Albion W. Tourgée, *A Fool's Errand and the Invisible Empire* (New York: Fords, Howard, and Hulbert, 1880).

[19] Tourgée, *A Fool's Errand* 164.

[20] Compare with Theodore Rosengarten's comment regarding the preparation of Ned Cobb's stories for publication: "I have not reproduced a southern or

black dialect because I did not hear it. I did hear the English language as I know it, spoken with regional inflection and grammar." Rosengarten xxiv.

[21] Tourgée, *A Fool's Errand* 165.

[22] Tourgée, *A Fool's Errand* 171, 359.

[23] Tourgée quoted in Current, *Those Terrible Carpetbaggers* 404.

[24] Tourgée quoted in Current, *Those Terrible Carpetbaggers* 405.

[25] Dixon's maternal uncle, attorney Leroy McAfee, helped to keep Ku Klux Klan a potent force in western North Carolina after the organization had disbanded in other parts of the state. Eric Foner, *Reconstruction: America's Unfinished Revolution, 1863–1877* (New York: Harper & Row, 1988) 433. Dixon's biographer is Raymond Allen Cook, *Fire from the Flint: The Amazing Careers of Thomas Dixon* (Winston-Salem, North Carolina: John F. Blair, Publisher, 1968). The lack of critical judgment in Cook's biography is displayed in his observations about Reconstruction, which are as crude and outdated as Dixon's.

[26] Quoted in Cook 13. In the "Author's Note" to *The Black Hood,* a novel that retold the Reconstruction experience in a later day of Klan resurgence, Dixon shortened the time he thought needed for an adequate view of the era: "The passing of a full half century from 1873 to 1923 has made it possible at last to see these events in their true perspective and record their significance." Thomas Dixon, Jr., *The Black Hood* (New York: D. Appleton and Company, 1924).

[27] Thomas Dixon, Jr., *The Leopard's Spots: A Romance of the White Man's Burden—1865–1900* (New York: Doubleday, Page & Company, 1902). That this novel did not reach bestseller status is based on the information offered in Alice Payne Hackett, *Fifty Years of Best Sellers, 1895–1945* (New York: R. R. Bowker Co., 1945) 18-21. Dixon's second novel, *The One Woman: A Story of Modern Utopia* (New York: Doubleday, Page & Company, 1903)—about the evils of socialism—sold better, making into the top ten bestsellers for 1903. His most famous novel, *The Clansman: An Historical Romance of the Ku Klux Klan* (New York: Doubleday, Page & Company, 1905), ranked fourth among bestsellers for 1905.

[28] Quoted in Cook 116.

[29] Dixon, *The Leopard's Spots* 333.

[30] Dixon, *The Leopard's Spots* 460.

[31] Thomas Dixon, *The Flaming Sword* (Atlanta, Georgia: Monarch Publishing Company, 1939) 11, 418–9. So greatly did W. E. B. Du Bois loathe the back-to-Africa message of Garvey that he wrote in *The Crisis* that "not even Tom Dixon" had "ever stooped to a more vicious campaign." W. E. B. Du Bois, "A Lunatic or a Traitor" in *Writings* (New York: The Library of America, 1986) 991.

[32] Dixon was able to arrange for private showings before the film's release to Wilson and his cabinet followed by Chief Justice Edward White, himself a former member of the Klan, and members of the Congress, all of which made it more difficult to prevent showings of the film once its sensational nature sparked controversy. Wilson concluded that the film was "like writing history with lightning," his only regret being "that it is all so terribly true." Quoted in Cook 170.

[33] W. E. B. Du Bois, *Dusk of Dawn* in *Writings* 730.

[34] Dixon, "To the Reader," *The Clansman*.

[35] Dixon, *The Clansman* 227, 310.

[36] Dixon, *The Clansman* 313–4, 316.

[37] Dixon, *The Clansman* 319, 323.

[38] White 789.

Chapter 7

Interpreting the Past with Light and Shadow

The daguerreotype is tarnished along its edges so that its image now ends jaggedly in silvery, graying triangles. The figures of its two young men, however, retain the eerie sharpness only this photographic process could achieve. The men are seated facing each other. Perhaps the daguerreotypist was the one who scratched names on the surface of the silvered and polished copper plate before putting it into a brass mat and under a piece of glass and setting it into an embossed, leather-covered wooden case. If so, we know that C. Jalers photographed Larry and Charley. The men appear by themselves, with lighted cigars their only props and no indication that the daguerreotype documented their occupations. The image, with its anonymity and formality, is typical of countless portraits made in the 1840s and 1850s; yet it is difficult to look at these individuals without pausing to wonder who they were and why they posed in that studio.

Both men are dressed similarly, with silk cravats, vests (trimmed in red by the daguerreotypist), frock coats, matching trousers, and large, soft hats. The effect is one of prosperity and is accentuated by the posture of Larry—if we assume the first name refers to the individual seated to the left. He is stretched back in his chair with his legs extended and crossed at the ankles, his right thumb in his vest pocket anchoring an arm akimbo, and his left hand prominently displaying his cigar. His open-lipped smile is unmistakable, good-natured, and striking since he must have held it for at least a minute while the exposure was made. As florid as the paisley vest he wears, Larry's bright countenance contrasts with Charley's, who seems to recede into the background as he sits in his chair cross-legged, his folded hands resting in his lap and his eyes peering out from under a hat pulled down low. His cigar is clenched in his mouth, leaving the viewer uncertain whether he is grimacing because of it or some unknown tension. He looks as if he would prefer to disappear into the shadows, retreating from his extroverted companion and, indeed, the viewer at whom he stares. Frozen in a time long past, the two have lost their ability to tell us whether they posed as brothers, business partners, or simply friends.

The daguerreotype of Larry and Charley was made on a sixth plate, measuring two-and-three-quarter inches by three-and-one-quarter inches, a common size once the daguerreotyping craze took root in the United States, where it flourished as nowhere else.[1] Its technology evolved rapidly and reached standardized practices soon after Louis Jacques Mandé Daguerre introduced the process in 1839, which built on the work of fellow Frenchman Joseph Nicéphore Niépce. Fashioning an image required a plate of copper that was thinly coated with silver and then cleaned and highly polished. Exposing the polished plate to iodine vapor made its surface sensitive to light and ready to be placed inside a light-proof holder and inserted into the camera. Once the plate was exposed, it was developed over fumes of hot mercury with the resulting image fixed by being immersed in a solution of sodium thiosulfate. Gilding with gold chloride finished the procedure, which resulted in a daguerreotype that, despite its fragility, left a remarkably permanent record.[2]

A daguerreotype is mesmerizing. Its silver surface reflects light like a mirror, and the reverse image it shows adds to its mirror-like quality. To be viewed, the daguerreotype must be tilted by the person holding it so that it reflects the image and not the viewer. The effect can be startling. Because of its sensitivity and high polish, the image is sharply and three-dimensionally defined, to a degree that one can still appreciate how stunning it must have been to have first beheld one a century and a half ago. While the fragility of the silvered plate required its casing in what soon became a decorative box, the daguerreotype's permanence as a record of its times also seems to mandate so composed a format.

This is not to say, however, that the daguerreotype was always admired by its subjects. In *Cold Mountain*, novelist Charles Frazier describes how Ada pulls from a drawer a photograph of Inman, her beloved who was wounded while fighting in the Confederate army. As she looked at the photograph, she remembered how her father, upon first seeing it, snapped the case shut and instead pulled from a shelf a volume of Ralph Waldo Emerson, reading aloud Emerson's reaction to his own daguerreotype:

> And in your zeal not to blur the image, did you not keep every finger in its place with such energy that your hands became clenched as for fight or despair, and in your resolution to keep your face still, did you not feel every moment more rigid; the brows contracted into a Tartarean frown,

and the eyes fixed as they are fixed in a fit of madness, or death?[3]

The quotation is taken from a journal entry written by Emerson in 1841, omitting the final line that summarizes how Emerson regarded daguerreotyping: "Could you not by grasping it very tight hold the stream of a river, or of a small brook, and prevent it from flowing?"[4] Emerson was objecting not only to how sitting still for a daguerreotype distorted one's features; he also discountenanced its attempt to capture life with a moment's exposure. The frozen moment, however, is precisely why the daguerreotype is so appealing. Of course the medium cannot capture life itself, and, to be understood, necessitates that its images be interpreted. Considering the photograph and its relationship to the culture that produced it, however, provides the viewer with a sense of having stepped midstream into a past moment.[5]

"Reading" the daguerreotype forces a recognition of how the daguerreotype's technology informed its practice, which reflected, in turn, the mores of its era. Because the daguerreotype was not made with the informality and ease of a snapshot, it also assumed something of a portrait's or a landscape's composed nature. "For this reason," writes Alan Trachtenberg, "the past we gain access to is not a 'pure' objective truth, but a truth already processed and reprocessed by human intention and mechanical limitation."[6] There is more here, therefore, than an artifact taken from the progress of photography; the daguerreotype also serves as a historical document offering insight into its era.

The daguerreotype of Larry and Charley is one of a personal collection of six historical photographs that I ask my students to examine as they consider the relationship between technology, culture, and the fashioning of identity. The second image in this collection is of a woman whose photograph—the word "photography" was first used to describe this process—is an ambrotype (from the Greek word for "immortal").[7] Developed in the early 1850s and quickly superseding the daguerreotype, the wet-plate or collodion method for making an ambrotype resulted in a negative image fixed on glass which was then blackened to make the image appear positive.[8] Unlike a daguerreotype, the ambrotype does not reverse its image. Although the glass plate could be cracked, as is this one, the new photography could be performed more cheaply and easily. Nevertheless, it had its critics, including one who complained that the silvery brilliance of the daguerreotype was being supplanted by the "black, nasty, filthy, ghastly, dead, inanimate, flat, shade of shadows."[9] The woman of this ambrotype is past middle age and is wearing a dark dress accented by a broach worn at the neck. Despite its overall effect of darkness, the image is clear enough to show that the book on which she is resting her arm has printed on its spine, "Patent Office Report 1855"!

Modifying the ambrotype method by spreading the collodion on a thin sheet of japanned iron created ferrotypes, more commonly known by the misnomer "tintype," which were produced cheaply well into the twentieth century. Five grown sisters posing with their mother in the last quarter of the nineteenth century (and sharing her dowdy expression) are the subject of the third photograph students scrutinize. (The one daughter bearing the hint of a smile is also the only one not dressed in solid, dark colors. Her lightly colored dress features two rows of buttons each of which is nearly two inches in diameter.) The ferrotype is nearly pristine, evidencing the technology's sturdiness and durability.

Mass production of photographs was made easier in the 1850s with the carte-de-visite, which corresponded to the dimensions of popular calling cards. A carte-de-visite was printed on stiff paper on which light-sensitive silver salt had been affixed with an albumen solution, multiple copies simultaneously recording with a camera having four lenses. As an example of this process, students view a photograph of a woman whose dress, age, and appearance closely resemble the ambrotype's subject.

Were these women posing without the men of their lives as an assertion of identity, or were these photographs perhaps made for loved ones, camped on fields of war in the 1860s? Other frequently encountered examples of cartes-de-visite show people dressed in the less refined clothing of working classes, an indication that the photograph's affordability affected how people saw themselves in quite literal ways. The social effect of this new availability was recognized at the time the image of the woman was made:

> Cartes de Visite are a curious study. Twelve months ago they were almost unknown: now they fill one or more volumes on every center table, and overshadow the contents of every card-basket.
>
> There must be a secret connected with this sudden and astonishing popularity, and this secret, undoubtedly, is self-love.[10]

Self-love, perhaps, but surely in a gentler way than the manner in which our more intensely narcissistic age would understand it, for the examples that most commonly have survived today tend to show plain people plainly posed.

The back of this carte-de-visite reveals almost as much as its front: H. C. Vansyckel's Photographic Sky-Light Gallery at No. 532 North Second Street in Philadelphia promised to retain negative 12926 to furnish duplicates for one year. In addition, a two-cent federal revenue stamp was affixed, canceled by the photographer's initials and the date "1866" written across it. As the result of a luxury tax enacted by the Congress in 1864, photographs were taxed for a two-year period, from 1864 to 1866, at a rate that varied depending on the price of the photograph. A two-cent stamp meant that the photograph had cost twenty-five cents, as cheaply as one could be made then. To show that the tax had been paid, the photographer affixed a revenue stamp which he then canceled by initialing and dating the stamp, thereby providing later generations with documentary information about the photographer that was otherwise frequently lost. Here, then, is a striking intersection of technology, consumer demand, and public policy. Demand for photographs of political and military leaders soared during the Civil War, fostered by a technology capable of meeting it with such ability that it also became a convenient source of revenue for a federal government making previously unimaginable expenditures.

The quality of the carte-de-visite, however, pales when compared to the cabinet card photograph of the late nineteenth century. So named because its size and appearance made it suitable for display in the home, the cabinet card marked a high point in popular studio photography. With the cabinet card, photography no longer had to rely on the wet plates of the collodion process; instead, a dry plate coated with gelatin which contained light-sensitized chemicals greatly reduced the time required for an exposure. Often edged in gold and printed with an ornately patterned advertisement as a backing, cabinet cards are still found at flea markets piled on tables where the browser quickly realizes that personal identity was rooted in a knowing and caring family, as the majority of the photographs fail to label their subject for outsiders. One such photograph was made in a studio in Allegan, Michigan, and shows a young girl clothed in a manner appropriate for celebrating the nation's centennial in 1876. Her dress includes a blouse ruffled at the neck and cuffs, a vest fastened with a long row of metal buttons, embossed possibly with an eagle, and a short jacket that sports facings and cuffs displaying the same buttons.

Each of the five photographs described here which I show my students was made in a studio. The sixth, while also posed, evidences the informality and candidness of a snapshot. It was taken by an amateur photographer wielding a camera that used celluloid film, such as was developed by George Eastman with his 1889 introduction of roll film. Now yellowing and with some of the details fading from view, the image is of six young women and five young men (the sixth man holding the camera?) who sit on the steps of a cottage numbered "23" at the front door. A few of the men are wearing jeans, as is at least one of the women; a bow tie and four-in-hand are also sported. Two of the men have been smoking, judging from the pipes they hold. Around the corner of the cottage sits a carriage. Unlike all the other photographs in the collection, this one is inscribed: "The Camping Party that occupied the Catalpa Cottage at Bennetts' Springs July, 1908. *Talk about fun we sure had it.* I shall never forget that trip. Elizabeth Taylor." A trip never to be forgotten—perhaps the photographic record helped to fix the trip in the writer's mind. A letter or diary detailing the vacation is absent, but the photograph with its simple inscription was apparently evocative enough to warrant its preservation.[11]

Considered as a collection, these six photographs provide a useful overview of one technology's progress, beginning with the striking but difficult to produce daguerreotype and ending with the cheap yet popularly accessible snapshot. Here is a technology that stretches backward in time surprisingly close to the nation's origins, with early daguerreotypes rendering the visages of aged veterans of the Revolutionary War.[12] Paralleling the nation's growth, photography as a technological process underwent industrial standardization that resulted in its becoming the common people's portraiture. As it developed into a truly portable process requiring little skill to operate, photography assumed an air of naturalness that made it an expected part of an excursion even into the backwoods of Bennetts' Springs. If one wants to model the way a technology develops, photography offers an example sufficiently compact in its time span and clearly enough demarcated in its advances to suggest a pattern that might be usefully applied to describe other technology's evolutions.

To treat technology separately from the culture that generates it, however, risks trivializing knowledge and fragmenting the past into pieces that do not connect with the present. So, if the first lesson taken from this collection of photographs is about the evolution of the technology, the second is that the frozen moment of the photograph documents the past, both directly, in its portrayal of people and events, and indirectly, as in the example of the carte-de-visite which was taxed to help finance a war effort—itself evidence of how deeply entrenched the photograph was in middle-class sensibilities. Students' attention now turns to the captured moment as a window opening into the past.

The captured moment can be seized by studio photographs, as students realize when carefully studying images commonly found in history texts. Consider, for example, the quarter-plate daguerreotype of Abraham Lincoln, his first ever, and attributed to Nicholas H. Shepherd and made in 1846 or 1847 before the newly elected congressman left Springfield, Illinois, for the nation's capital.[13] Dressed and groomed more neatly than he ever again appeared in a photograph, Lincoln sits primly with his right elbow resting on a book and his muscular left hand folded on his leg. His appearance is of a country lawyer only recently acquainted with the clothes required of his profession, determined to show supporters and critics alike that his abilities match his ambition. All the while he shows the trace of a smile—maybe self-deprecating, or barely masking the rowdy, wry humor he frequently indulged in. It is, perhaps, the most straightforwardly honest of all his many photographs in its correspondence to the way he was regarded by his contemporaries, exceeded for its directness only by his last one, taken four days before Lincoln's death in April 1865.

As photographer Alexander Gardner developed this image in his Washington, D. C., studio, the glass plate negative cracked, and Gardner made only one albumen print before discarding it.[14] The resulting line that runs through Lincoln's hair only adds to the poignancy of the portrait, which shows a man nearly unrecognizable when compared to the daguerreotype of eighteen years earlier. Now, the lined and hollow face of the fifty-six-year-old President reflects the weariness brought by a war he had described in biblical terms for its judgmental destructiveness, while his serene smile suggests a great work now done. Not only is his coarse hair more familiarly unkempt, it is also graying, as is his severely clipped beard. The day of the photograph had been a busy one for the President, attending both to routine matters and to special gatherings as the city began to noisily celebrate Lee's surrender to Grant at Appomattox, but it must also have been a deeply satisfying one as well.[15]

Taken as a pair, the daguerreotype and the albumen print provide students with historical documents that they can "read," inwardly, for biographical evidence, and outwardly, for what the photographs reveal of its times, subject to the limitations that the technology imposes. (To what extent, for example, is the stiffness of the daguerreotype's pose due to the requirements of its lengthy exposure?) The moment frozen in the photographer's studio insists upon more than description; it also urges the viewer to interpret what is seen along with what can be known in the larger historical context. In short, students are called upon to make the past memorable by entering it and imagining living presences within it.

Outside of the studio, the effect of the captured moment can be even more dramatic. There are photographs of such immediate presence that they are almost embarrassingly frank, as if the viewer and photographer are uninvited, maybe even unwelcome, guests. Such a feeling was reported by Yoshito Matsushige, a thirty-two-year-old cameraman for *Chugoku Shimbun*, the Hiroshima daily newspaper, who staggered toward the hypocenter soon after the atomic bombing on August 6, 1945. Unable to pass beyond the Miyuki Bridge because of the fireballs sweeping from out of the city center, Matsushige was stunned by the sight of the people, many of whom were junior high girls from two nearby schools, who had gathered at the bridge and were suffering with blistering burns that left their flesh peeling from their bodies. Although he had come into the city for the purpose of taking photographs, Matsushige was confronted by "such a hellish apparition" that he almost lacked the will to do so: "I hesitated for about twenty minutes before I finally pushed it [the camera shutter] and took this first picture." Years after this photograph was recognized for its rare documentation of the immediate aftermath of the atomic bombing, Matsushige described the image:

> The man in the picture might be a policeman giving first aid to people for burns using cooking oil. A can of oil's there. This woman's hair was burned frizzy. They were all barefoot because their shoes had stuck to the asphalt. This woman was holding a baby in the crook of her arm. She was half naked. The baby's eyes were closed. Either dead or in shock. She was running around crying to her child, "Please open your eyes." The baby was probably already dead. You can see in the picture that her legs are slightly blurred. The film was slow then, so you can tell she was running.[16]

"Taking" a photograph in this context assumed a new significance that helps to explain Matsushige's hesitation: to those from whom everything else had just been taken, including even a recognizable humanity, it seemed a horrible thing to be standing around and snapping photographs. As it was, Matsushige could take only five of them. "I'm often asked why I didn't take more pictures," Matsushige remarked. "Some even criticize me for that. It makes me angry. How can they ask such a thing? They didn't see the reality. It was too overwhelming."[17] Matsushige's photograph of the people gathered at the Miyuki Bridge less than three hours after the atomic bombing possesses an immediacy that even the remembrances of the *hibakusha* ("a-bomb victims") do not. As close as we come by way of this photograph to the dark-skied, burning city and its stunned and dying people, Matsushige's comment about not seeing the reality reminds us of the past's fleetness. The caution to the history student is that even the most dramatic photographs do not "capture" anything except light and shadow, and that it is the power of our imaginations, tempered by the limitations of our knowledge, that allow us to know the past.

A more intentionally composed image, however, still retains an ability to move the viewer with a sense of time past. A second well-known and unique image my students view is a half-plate daguerreotype made in the afternoon of August 22, 1850, in the central New York town of Cazenovia, located near the Peterboro estate of philanthropist and abolitionist Gerrit Smith. The event was the Cazenovia Fugitive Slave Law Convention, called on the eve of the enactment of one of the most bitterly contested laws in American history: the Fugitive Slave Act of 1850, fiercely denounced by its opponents because it required the participation of federal marshals in the arrest and return of runaway slaves. At the heart of the debate over the bundle of legislative initiatives that included the Fugitive Slave Act was the question of whether southern states were so unalterably opposed to any attempt to limit the expansion of slavery into the western territories taken in the Mexican War that they would attempt to secede from the Union if they thought their right to slaveholding was being jeopardized. Frederick Douglass had already debated Smith earlier that year in Syracuse, New York, arguing that southerners would be unable to maintain control of their slaves without the northern military power they would lose in a secession movement.[18]

By the time of the Cazenovia convention, Douglass (who presided) was exercising his growing influence as a financially secure newspaper editor—thanks in measure to Smith's support—to aid runaways fleeing to Canada, speak at the first national woman's rights convention, and address the American Anti-Slavery Society's annual meeting in New York City, even at risk to his personal safety. Not long after the convention, he informed Smith that he would no longer assume, along with southern slaveholders, that the Constitution in its intent blessed slavery; instead, he would argue—to the surprise of abolitionists like William Lloyd Garrison—that the language of the Constitution's Preamble contained the idealism necessary to completely undermine the South's "peculiar institution."[19]

This ferment of activity is pictured in the Cazenovia convention daguerreotype as if it were one of the participants.[20] Taken outdoors and framed with the trees of Grace Wilson's orchard, Douglass is seated on a platform at the end of a table where Theodosia Gilbert (wearing bloomers) and abolitionist Joseph Hathaway wield quill pens, presumably transcribing an account of the proceedings. At the center of the image, standing behind and to one side of Douglass, is Gerrit Smith, so close an associate and friend that Douglass would dedicate to him his second autobiography, *My Bondage and My Freedom*, in 1855. Surrounding Smith and Douglass are men and women, black and white, including the two teenage girls and runaway slaves Mary and Emily Edmonson. Smith's extended arms present the platform guests as the daguerreotype's viewer looks over the heads of the audience and is clearly welcomed into the formally yet naturally posed scene.

It is a remarkable image. Unlike the others used in class, this one features famous people seemingly interrupted in carrying out their momentous actions, among which was the writing of the "Letter to the American Slaves" urging slaves to resort to violence if necessary in their efforts to escape. If students seek evidence that events are shaped by individuals, this daguerreotype lends credence to the argument. Its placement of speakers, guests, secretaries, and audience give it an appealing directness that typifies an era of benevolent associations dedicated to reform of all kinds. The occasion it marks adds an urgency that would make it as appropriate an instrument of propaganda as of commemoration.[21] Its artfulness results from its artlessness and contrasts sharply with the last in this set of three famously dramatic photographs, a photograph made three-quarters of a century after the Cazenovia daguerreotype and more subtly artful in its composition and intense in its message.

Dorothea Lange was one of a host of photographers employed by the Resettlement Administration (later the Farm Security Administration) to help with the public relations effort to win support for Franklin Roosevelt's New Deal agricultural programs, by providing photographs documenting living conditions of the poorest, most dislocated farmers of the Great Depression. The huge picture file created by her and her colleagues through the early 1940s was eventually given to the Library of Congress for preservation and study, where much of it can be accessed today as easily as visiting the Library's web site.

The collection of pictures, largely taken with black-and-white film, creates so powerful an image of the Depression years that it can come as a surprise to remember that the 1930s occurred in color! Many of the pictures became classic images of American hard times—anonymous men with their heads dropped in despair as they wait in an unemployment line; a father and his sons running for cover in an Oklahoma dust storm; migrants huddled in old cars with possessions strapped to the sides. One picture, however, emerges as iconic: Dorothea Lange's 1936 *Migrant Mother*.

Lange's 1960 account of how this picture came to be is prosaic.[22] She said that she had wanted to drive past a migrant peapickers camp in Nipomo, California, on a rainy afternoon in March 1936 so that she could return home by late that evening. Instead, she stopped, "following instinct, not reason," and soon

> saw and approached the hungry and desperate mother, as if drawn by a magnet. I do not remember how I explained my presence or my camera to her, but I do remember she asked me no questions. I made five exposures, working closer and closer from the same direction. I did not ask her name or her history. She told me her age, that she was 32. She said that they had been living on frozen vegetables from the surrounding fields, and birds that the children killed. She had just sold the tires from her car to buy food. There she sat in that lean-to with her children huddled around her, and seemed to know that my pictures might help her, and so she helped me. There was a sort of equality about it.[23]

Prosaic perhaps unfairly characterizes Lange's description which, despite its brevity, conveys much of the attitudes of the New Deal. The subject, as Lange knew from her notes, was Florence Thompson, a widow with seven children. Leaving her nameless made her an archetype for the desperation that confronted migrant workers. Her desperation, however, was not beyond remedy, which presumably would soon come from a sympathetic government able to recognize her humanity, her equality, her simple need.

Lange took six pictures of Thompson and her children that afternoon.[24] The first two are from far enough away that Lange was able to fit the entire lean-to in the frame. The third comes closer, but remains sufficiently distant to show a large, empty tin plate resting on an old wooden box. The last three come closer, with one showing Thompson nursing an infant. It is the last picture that became one of the most widely reproduced images of the American Depression. In it, Thompson shares the frame with only three of her children—the infant now asleep and, at each of their mother's shoulders, two older children with their faces turned away, perhaps in bashfulness as Lange moved closer. Their pose emphasizes Thompson's pained, far-off look that is further accentuated by the tentative, despairing way her hand is held at her cheek.

Lange's genius lay in avoiding cynical manipulation by creating an image laden with meaning at many levels—depending on whether the pictures are viewed separate from one another as symbols of the period or collectively as an exercise in photographic journalism; with or without Lange's observations; in the context of how they were understood by the New Deal or the general public; from an artist or a historian's point of view. "Rather than as a measure of an objective reality," concludes Alan Trachtenberg, "indicating what exists in the world, photographs are better thought of as a means of representation. . . . The final danger is to see any photograph as fixed and final, either in order, meaning, or time and place."[25]

What, then, is required of students who enter the worlds of charred Hiroshima, sunny Cazenovia, rainy Nipomo? With the personal collection of six photographs, there were few limitations on what students could read into the images before them. By contrast, these three pictures have a documented past which, to be fair to the past, must be taken into account. That said, their interpretation remains with us in the present, where we can find multiple meanings in them. Students who are encouraged to study these images as more than mere illustrations for a printed text are better able to engage in the dialogue that exists between past and present. Considering how attuned today's youth are to visual images, the photograph is an easily accessible and appropriate place from which to begin an inquiry into historical culture, its technology, and those messages which have survived to the present.

One final point brings full circle this consideration of utilizing photographs in the classroom. The selections brought to class form a metaphor for the search for identity. (Ironically, Yoshito Matsushige noted that he had been criticized for not taking *more* pictures, to better identify a new class of Japanese citizenry, the *hibakusha*.) This is not to imply that the need for self-presentation arose only in the nineteenth century, but that the advent of photography opened new possibilities for fashioning identity. As Alain Corbin suggests, "The ability to portray the self and the possession of self-images enhanced the individual's sense of his own importance and democratized the need to stake out a social position."[26] Not surprisingly photography has flourished in a nation in which welcomed social leveling also effected an unwelcome erosion of personal distinctions. So ubiquitous are photographs in our time that I ask students to conclude our survey by bringing to class a favorite photograph of themselves, one that will satisfy the considerations we have raised in class: a photograph as a personal memento, a social document, a captured moment. Few of the homework assignments I make are as engaging for students as this one. My expectation is that we will share what they bring to class in light of what we have learned from our careful examination of the historical record; my hope is that we will have also made it easier to learn from one another.

Notes

[1] Beaumont Newhall, *The Daguerreotype in America* (New York: Dover Publications, Inc., 1976) 36.

[2] This process is described with more technical detail in M. Susan Barger and William B. White, *The Daguerreotype: Nineteenth-Century Technology and Modern Science* (Washington, D. C.: Smithsonian Institution Press, 1991) 44–6. The Library of Congress's "American Memory" web site also offers a concise description of daguerreotype technology at its digital exhibit "America's First Look into the Cameria: Daguerreotype Portraits and Views, 1839–1862," 27 November 27 1997, <http://lcweb2.loc.gov/ammem/daghtml/daghome.html> (16 February 1998).

[3] Charles Frazier, *Cold Mountain* (New York: Atlantic Monthly Press, 1997) 194.

[4] The journal entry, dated 24 October 1841, is quoted in Newhall 76–7.

[5] Alan Trachtenberg seeks "an intelligible view of society implicit in the internal dialogue of images and text, and their external dialogue with their times," in *Reading American Photographs: Images as History, Mathew Brady to Walker Evans* (New York: Hill and Wang, 1989). The quotation appears on p. xv.

[6] National Archives Trust Fund Board, *The American Image: Photographs from the National Archives, 1860–1960*, intro. Alan Trachtenberg (New York: Pantheon Books, 1979) xxix.

[7] Newhall 65.

[8] "Collodion" refers to the guncotton (nitrocellulose) and potassium iodide solution that was sensitized with silver nitrate and used to coat the photographic plate. After exposure, the image was developed by being washed with pyrogallic acid and silver iodide, being finally fixed with sodium thiosulphate. Newhall 65, 107.

[9] J. H. Fitzgibbon wrote his complaint in 1861 and is quoted in Newhall 108.

[10] "Cartes-de-Visite," *Humphrey's Journal* 1 October 1862: 123–4 quoted in Steve Knoblock, ed., "Cartes de Visites: A Social Revolution," <http://www.webcom/cityg/earlyphoto/articles/Cartes_de_Visite_A_Social_Revolution. html> (16 March 1998).

[11] Emphasis in the original. The inscription perhaps refers to Bennett Spring State Park, known for its camping, hiking, boating, swimming, and rainbow trout fishing opportunities along the Niangua River in the Missouri Ozarks. See Henry G. Alsberg, ed., *The American Guide: A Source Book and Complete Travel Guide for the United States* (New York: Hastings House, 1949) 620.

[12] See, for example, the images of David Kinnison, who took part in the Boston Tea Party; Peter Stephen Du Ponceau, who served as aide-de-camp to Major General the Baron von Steuben; and Albert Gallatin, who immigrated to America in 1780 and was President Jefferson's treasury secretary, in Smithsonian Books, *Images of America: A Panorama of History in Photographs* (Washington, D. C.: Smithsonian Books, 1989) 18–9.

[13] The daguerreotype (with its companion one of Mary Lincoln) is found in the Library of Congress Prints and Photograph Division, call number DAG no. 1224.

[14] The print is found in the National Portrait Gallery, Smithsonian Institution, accession number NPG.81.M1.

[15] The events surrounding 10 April 1865, the day when Lincoln last visited Alexander Gardner, who photographed five poses at that sitting, are recounted in David Herbert Donald, *Lincoln* (New York: Simon and Schuster, 1995) 580–3, and Benjamin P. Thomas, *Lincoln: A Biography* (New York: Alfred A. Knopf, 1952) 513–5.

[16] Matsushige's account appears in Haruko Taya Cook and Theodore F. Cook, *Japan at War: An Oral History* (New York: The New Press, 1992) 391–5. Matsushige was also interviewed by the Hiroshima Peace Cultural Center and NHK, the public broadcasting company of Japan, for the film *Hiroshima Witness*. A transcript of his comments is available at the web site "Voice of Hibakusha," 22 April 1994, <http://129.171.129.67/mf/hibakusha/index. html> (15 April 1998). The photograph has been printed in The Committee for the Compilation of Materials on Damage Caused by the Atomic Bombs, ed., *Hiroshima and Nagasaki: The Physical, Medical, and Social Effects of the Atomic Bombings* (New York: Basic

Books, Inc., Publishers, 1981) ii.

[17] Cook and Cook 395.

[18] Frederick Douglass, *Autobiographies* (New York: Library of America, 1994) 1059.

[19] Douglass described what he termed "this radical change" in his opinions in the chapter entitled, "Triumphs and Trials," in his third autobiography, *Life and Times of Frederick Douglass* (1893) 703–7.

[20] Details about the daguerreotype are taken from a local history that has unraveled questions about its origin and identified many of the individuals appearing in it. See Hugh C. Humphreys, "'Agitate! Agitate! Agitate!': The Great Fugitive Slave Law Convention and Its Rare Daguerreotype." *Madison County Heritage* 19 (Oneida, New York: Madison County Historical Society, 1994).

[21] Humphreys proposes that the reason Gilbert is seated at the platform table, even though she had no official role in the proceedings, is that the daguerreotype was to be given to her fiancé, William Chaplin of the New York Anti-Slavery Society, who, at the time of the convention, was imprisoned in the District of Columbia for attempting to aid in the escape of two slaves belonging to Georgia congressmen Robert Toombs and Alexander H. Stephens. Humphreys 10–1, 40–1.

[22] Dorothea Lange, "The Assignment I'll Never Forget," *Popular Photography* 46, no. 2 (February 1960): 42–3, 126.

[23] Lange 126.

[24] The entire series of photographs is reproduced in Carl Fleischhauer and Beverly W. Brannan, ed., *Documenting America, 1935–1943* (Berkeley: University of California Press, 1988) 16–7. *Migrant Mother* is nicely reproduced in larger size on p. 69. The original and negative reside in the Library of Congress, call number LC–USZ62–95653.

[25] Alan Trachtenberg, "From Image to Story," in Fleischhauer and Brannan 70.

[26] Alain Corbin, "Backstage," in Michelle Perrot, ed., *A History of Private Life*, vol. IV, *From the Fires of Revolution to the Great War* (Cambridge, Massachusetts: The Belknap Press of Harvard University Press, 1990) 463. Corbin also addresses other consequences of the advent of photography that go unmentioned

here: the demand for pornographic photographs and the use of photography by police to fix the identity of criminals.

Chapter 8

Reading Really Old Textbooks

History textbooks are difficult to love. They are like a friend more shallow than is first apparent. Initial attraction to bright colors and sophisticated layouts soon fades as it becomes clear that they never vary their stories or even their voice, but remain always unaware of their incompleteness. Even the best of them, unlike works of fiction, lack enough layering of meaning to hold the reader's attention. Perhaps it is different for students who have never seen the battered textbook just put into their hands, as it was put into the hands of other students in previous years, but I suspect that for them there are other off-putting factors at play.

Surely the most egregious of their failings is that a textbook's choppy paragraphs rarely develop into a narrative line. Instead, they are stuffed with facts and strung together into sections that end with lists of recall questions—even textbooks used in elementary schools, where storytelling is still part of the school day, are this way. Sensitive teachers learn to use textbooks like encyclopedias, referred to when necessary, and abandon with regret the notion that they can be storybooks. Perhaps stories require of a curriculum stuffed with goals, objectives, and measurements too much time and allow for too many alternative understandings to exist comfortably in schools.

Stories make no pretense to objectivity, which renders them suspect for a profession as pervaded by scientism as education is today. Such, however, was not always the case, especially in the early years of this country when the common school movement took root. Then, textbooks often told stories and were fairly explicit in the values conveyed, with concomitant, unstated assumptions found not far from the surface. They had the most powerful motivations for being this way, and one that we should be able to appreciate: the present was quickly unfolding in a manner that promised to obliterate the cherished ways of the past. Awareness of the values contained in historical textbooks makes for a richer understanding of the past and a sharpened judgment better able to perceive the culture's values today.

Students today become critical readers by sensitizing themselves to the values and assumptions encountered in "safe" texts, that is, ones that are so removed from the present that carefully examining them does not threaten the status quo. Reading textbooks of the common school era critically reminds us of the complaint that modern education is no longer interested in the pursuit of moral values (it is, of course, but not the values recognized or desired by its critics). My hope in asking students to read selections from these textbooks is that they will learn to more readily identify the moral messages they provide, not to thoughtlessly reject them, but to evaluate their claims and more clearly consider issues of unity and diversity. Such examination, of course, risks dissent, but this trait is as much a part of our cultural inheritance as is babbitry, and I know of no better way to stifle the cheap cynicism that says our ideals are only hollow words, than by identifying values earnestly held and asking how well they were maintained.

Fortunately, the textbooks of the common school are not too difficult to find in second-hand bookstores or university libraries (assuming they have not been purged as no longer relevant for students by those who think no earlier generation has been compelled to struggle with questions of identity). A small collection of these textbooks, drawn especially from the many series of readers and histories, provides a ready resource for study. A good beginning point involves considering the relationship between the textbooks and their cultural milieu.

Common schools and their textbooks grew into a major reform movement during a period of national fervor that followed the War of 1812, which had a simultaneous sense that the nation was losing touch with its origins. Of all the bewildering transformations that gripped the youthful United States during the Jacksonian years, one was of great symbolic significance. The generation that had led the Revolution was gone. Its two patriarchs, John Adams and Thomas Jefferson, died within hours of each other on the day of the Declaration of Independence's fiftieth anniversary. Their passing left a lone signer of the Declaration: Charles Carroll of Carrollton, Maryland, who, before his own death in 1832, lived long enough to play a role in the founding of the Baltimore and Ohio Railroad. Years later, when Abraham Lincoln spoke of the "mystic cords of memory, stretching from every battle-field, and patriot grave, to every living heart and hearthstone, all over this broad land," he voiced a concern central to educators facing the demands of industrialization, immigration, and westward expansion. How could this generation, now removed from the one of the founding fathers, keep the political, social, and economic values found in the Declaration of Independence?[1]

One way to conserve and transmit these values was through the textbooks that were adopted by the rapidly growing common school movement. Although the series of McGuffey Readers would dominate the field by the end of the nineteenth century, the choice facing educators fifty years earlier was as wide open as might be expected in so new an enterprise.[2] Indeed, the federal census of 1860 shows that the $5,500,000 worth of schoolbooks produced that year to be nearly half of the total value of all books manufactured and sold in the nation during the previous decade.[3] Nevertheless, despite the variety of titles, the textbooks make clear the ideology of the common school movement. In the advocacy of a civic morality based on virtue, of a patriotism embodying the belief of America's special destiny under the care of a beneficent God, and of a vision of a social order insuring success for all who were hardworking and honest, the textbooks of the common school movement offered a vision of the nation's future as real to its leaders as were the sentiments embodied in the Declaration of Independence to its authors.[4]

There is a difference, of course, between how these books are used in the classroom for evidence of the cultural values they carried and how they would be appropriated by a historian seeking to understand the common school movement. Several factors, for example, limit the completeness of a classroom examination, and remembering these limitations serves as a reminder of the discipline required of a historian. The most obvious one affects any study involving artifacts: the survival of some books and not others may distort the historical record and obfuscate issues of availability and regional difference in what was selected to be read. A second limiting factor involves the question of the accessibility of books in schools not endowed with rich financial support. The sentiment expressed in 1850 by Martha Rogers, teaching in Caseville, Missouri, was likely shared by many others: "I would like very much to have this coming session a class in Physiology & one in United States History, but cannot obtain the books."[5] Lastly, the demands of keeping order in a one-room school filled with rambunctious children of all ages raises the suspicion that any textbook ideology was less important than the mechanics of demonstrating literacy for a teacher too harried to emphasize notions of virtue or attitudes toward the poor. In an 1853 letter to

Nancy Swift of the National Popular Education Board, Cynthia Bishop described her school day routine in New Durham, Indiana:

> I have an hour & a half intermission, then the little ones read, classes in Peter Parley's & Mitchell's recite, the older scholars spell, & we have a few minutes to devote to miscellaneous exercises, which have excited so much interest that they have been willing to *shorten* the recess as a means of *prolonging* them. This I do not do, except occasionally.[6]

Values "learned" in such rote fashion may not have affected student behavior in ways desired by the educators writing the textbooks. For the students in my classroom, however, historiographic issues like these, while worth raising, are less important than the awareness that an era's textbooks are a conduit for transmitting a culture's values. That a culture should think of preserving itself—never mind whether or not its values are worth preserving—is a new idea to many students and often awakens them to the idea that the culture may have messages to instill even when the students are not aware of them.

That the physical presence of an old textbook has the power to evoke wonderment about the student who first held it is not a new observation. Lucia B. Downing related a poignant scene from her experience as a teacher which began in 1882 when, remarkably, she was only fourteen years old herself. One morning at the schoolhouse, a new pupil appeared, "a young lady in trailing gown," who was even older than her new teacher.

> She brought with her a little purple primer, with such lucid and inspiring sentences as, 'Lo, I go! See me go up.' She had learned to read out of that antiquated book before I was born, but in the interviewing years reading had become a lost art, and she was ready to begin all over. It was a wonderful help to me in killing time, never too often to please her, as she stood by me and picked out the sentences, letter by letter.[7]

One wonders about this young lady with the little purple primer. What faith she must have had in the printed word to save a book that had no practical value in her life, long after she had lost the ability even to read it. The book, we know by its language, was old—did it have written on its fly leaf the names of siblings who had successively passed it on to younger ones as they mastered its lessons? Did the contents excite the woman's imagination with tales drawn from the Bible or the Revolution? Did she find admonitions for her own behavior in a world in which the guidance of a mother may no longer have been available? We can only speculate whether, as she recited her lessons, the woman hoped to make the book's old-fashioned language her own, or whether the younger pupils regarded her as an object of ridicule or an inspiration for their studies. Holding such a dog-eared, torn, and unhinged book today, one is struck by how mute it is in so many ways about the hands that once held it, the eyes that scrutinized its pages, the tongue that recited its lessons, and the mind that held its own opinions about what was being taught.

Though mute in some ways, the textbooks of the common school movement clearly speak with an ideology that reflects the orientation of Protestant, native-born, capitalistic patriots. That being said, these textbooks did not lack their critics, especially when one remembers the era's emerging sectional differences. Horace Mann's dictum "that the classroom is neither the tribunal to adjudicate nor the forum to discuss" controversial issues did not mean that textbooks had escaped the growing controversy over slavery.[8] Not surprisingly, geography texts that compared the nation's regional differences were targeted for criticism, at least among southerners who were conscious of the fact that textbook authors tended to be New Englanders. Daniel Adams' *Geography*, first printed in Boston in 1819 with many subsequent editions, described the inhabitants of New England as being

> much engaged in commercial pursuits and in various manufactures. Great numbers find employment in the fisheries. The landholders are generally cultivators of the soil which they possess. Slavery is not known in New England.

As a result of these activities:

> The distribution of wealth is more equal here than in any other civilized country. The institutions of religion are well supported, and public schools, except in Rhode Island, are maintained by law, in every town. There is not another country on the globe, perhaps, where education is so generally diffused among all classes and order of citizens as in the New England States.[9]

This glowing description is paralleled by a less flattering one about the Southern states:

> About one third part of the whole number of the inhabitants in the low country are negro slaves. Labour here is thought disreputable for a white man. It is otherwise in the upper country. There, having but few slaves, labour is thought no disgrace, and the white people cultivate and manage their farms, much as in the New England States.[10]

The issue is not the fairness of the characterization. More striking is that the implied ideal is that of the New England farmer: shrewd, tenacious, honest, and untainted by the slothful and, therefore, sinful habit of slaveholding. As Southern paranoia increased in the years preceding the Civil War, such descriptions, with their hint of condescension, if not condemnation, proved intolerable. A widely reprinted 1860 editorial from the *Richmond Enquirer* declared:

> It is time that we were rid of Yankee school books. Ever since Morse published his Geography, in which there were flings at the institutions of the South, the school books of the North, which have flooded the South—in fact, we have no other school books—have been filled with Abolitionism, and if not with the outrageousness of Longfellow's anti-slavery cant, the books, nevertheless, squinted that way, and had the taint of Northern fanaticism in them. . . .
>
> We must stop the Northern inundation of school books. Have we not Southern men capable of compiling them?[11]

At the same time that sectional tensions were manifesting themselves in textbooks, a nationalistic fervor was also present, constituting an important part of textbook ideology. Needless to say, history texts offered the most florid panegyrics. The intense nationalism unleashed by the War of 1812 was supplemented in the 1840s with cries of the nation's "manifest destiny" to dominate the entire North American continent. Marcius Willson's *History of the United States* exemplified this national pride based on a belief in Providence's special blessing.[12] After a review of the previous sixty years' "progress," both in the nation's geographic expansion and economic development, Willson proclaims that the United States had reached a "vigorous manhood." Now, modern communication and transportation systems bound together more firmly the distant sections of the Union. These advances could not have been accomplished merely by the efforts of the citizenry:

> The Bible, and the institutions of Christianity, shed their blessings upon

> us; and the education of youth, upon which the well-being of society, and the perpetuity of our republican institutions, so greatly depend, is receiving that share of attention which its importance demands. For all these blessings we are bound to acknowledge and adore the invisible hand that has directed and sustained us; for every step in our progress has been distinguished by manifest tokens of providential agency.

Willson concludes with a prayer that the God who protected the settlers who had built "an empire in the wilderness" would continue to bless the nation that is now the world's hope of liberty. Then, alluding to the controversies presently splitting the Union, Willson urged:

> Let us endeavor to cultivate a spirit of mutual concession and harmony in our national councils; and remembering that the monarchies of the Old World are looking upon us with jealousy, and predicting the day of our ruin, let us guard with sacred faith the boon that has been bequeathed us, and amid all the turmoils of political strife by which we may be agitated, let us ever bear aloft the motto, '*The Union: one and inseparable.*'[13]

This last quotation, from Daniel Webster's ringing 1830 denunciation of the argument advanced by South Carolina senator Robert Y. Hayne (that the states possessed the power to nullify federal laws they deemed contrary to the Constitution), must have rankled many southerners. The best-known orator of his generation, and one whose conclusion to his reply to Hayne was recited by many school children, Webster's stand against secessionists illustrates how intertwined the strands of nationalism and sectionalism were, and how difficult it was for a textbook author to avoid controversy.

The greatest impression left by studying the common school's textbooks, however, is of the clarity and universality of their ideology. Using the term "ideology" to describe what textbooks wanted to teach does not mean to suggest that these beliefs were held by only a small group of reformers. The values inherent in the textbooks of the period would have struck much of their adult audience as based on shared, or "common," experiences of those who lived in a culture shaped by both the rationality of the Enlightenment and the evangelical fervor of the Great Awakenings. The proclamation on the cover page of Lyman Cobb's *Cobb's Sequel to the Juvenile Readers* is hardly unique in stating the book's purpose as being "to impress the minds of youth with sentiments of virtue and religion."[14] Such values would likely have gone unspoken if not for the challenges posed to them by the unforeseen consequences of immigration, industrialization, and a host of jarring reform movements which included new religious sects, feminism, and anti-slavery activity. Still, what is left assumed but unsaid in many of the stories told to children is just as striking. The stories that related the behaviors of boys and girls and men and women reveal much about how society expected individuals to fill the roles of husband, wife, parent, citizen, worker, young person, and old, rich, and poor. Two stories I have drawn from common school textbooks relate values both articulated and taken for granted and applied to two groups frequently not allowed to speak for themselves: women and the poor.

"Portrait of a Worldly Woman" appears in *Cobb's Sequel to the Juvenile Readers*. The setting is briefly drawn:

> A woman has spent her youth without the practice of any remarkable virtue, or the commission of anything which is flagrantly wrong; and she is now united with a man, whose moral endowments are not more distinguished than her own, but who is industrious, rich, and prosperous.[15]

Already, several points are made. Virtue comes through "practice," not necessarily by natural inclination. There can be little debate as to the woman's character: After all, the text's readers may have readily remembered how Christ had condemned the church of the Laodiceans for being "lukewarm, and neither cold nor hot."[16] The husband is "industrious" and, therefore, rich, but his economic status by itself is not sufficient for high praise. He has wealth, and the story soon adds that it is the wife who squanders it.

The "worldly woman" cared little for her religion. She attended church only because convention required it, and, therefore, she found it easy to miss services when she felt indisposed or the weather was inclement. Her attitude toward religion could not help but affect her children.

> Of domestick religion there is not even a semblance. As her husband does not think proper to pray with his family, so she does not think proper to pray with her children, or to instruct them in the doctrines and duties of Christianity.

Responsibilities for the spiritual upbringing of the children are thus delineated. As the management of all household activities naturally belonged to the wife, the worldly woman is further censured for indulging only herself and her family, "not that she may make a feast for the poor, the maimed, the lame, and the blind, but that she may make a dinner or a supper for her rich neighbors, who will bid her again." Even when, out of peer pressure, she gives something of herself to public charities, she does so grudgingly, "in the same light as her husband views the taxes which he pays to the government, as a debt which must be discharged, but from which she would be glad to escape." The implication seems to be that the discharge of a public duty should not be onerous, but the woman's averseness to service is clearly as important as whatever good her actions may have accomplished.[17]

The worldly woman's worst trait is her failure to temper her rationality in guarding her self-interest with a proper religious attitude about the well-being of the less fortunate. She offers a variety of reasons for declining to help the poor; she has no poor relations herself, for example, and the poor are so often "vicious" and fail to demonstrate the proper gratitude for what is done for them. After all, she thinks,

> They have little regard to truth; and, although it must be allowed that their distress is not altogether imaginary, yet they are ever disposed to exaggerate their sufferings. While they are ready to devour one another, they are envious toward the rich, and the kindness of their benefactors they commonly repay with ingratitude.[18]

How should this woman have behaved? The lesson demands neither an examination of attitudes about the poor nor an investigation of why the poor are so numerous. Rather, the worldly woman forgot that "the Christian woman, who sincerely loves God and her neighbor, in imitation of her heavenly Father, is kind to the evil as well as the good, to the unthankful as well as the grateful."[19] Patronizing attitudes about the poor are left unchallenged, but the attitude of a woman who failed in her Christian duty showing charity is not.

The idea of a civic responsibility flowing out of a Christian morality rests uncomfortably in today's culture, which has largely defined obligations toward the poor (insofar as they are still defined) on a more secular basis. Reading this story in the classroom today reinforces the past's strangeness, but also informs students of the energy that built much of this nation. To the extent that it assumes a cultural homogeneity that did not necessarily exist, these old textbooks also inadvertently raise the issue of how common schools might have been regarded by those who did not share in their outlook. How would, for example, a poor Irish immigrant worker, or an African-American, or a crusader for women's rights have understood the story's appeal to Christian charity? For today's student, however, for whom the textbook appears only as a tedious compendium of minutiae, there is also an example of how the book is constructed in ways that convey the interests and concerns of the culture in which they are expected to be read. Those students who learn to read between the lines can better judge for themselves both the strengths and weaknesses of the society they are entering and preparing to help lead.

This story reflects badly on an adult, leaving one to wonder whether it would have caused unwelcome domestic discord if a student were too quick to recognize his or her own parents in it. More often, common school textbooks wove their moral teachings into settings involving children. One example which evokes life in the schoolroom is "Sophia's Victory," which is recounted in Charles W. Sanders' *Union Reader, Number Three,* one in an extensive series of textbooks.[20] Sophia Lawton was poor; her clothes attested to her circumstances. Nevertheless, she is the heroine of the story, and, as if to emphasize her worthiness, the story notes that her poverty resulted not from shiftlessness but from a father who was dead and a mother unable to pay her tuition. Charity to Sophia, however, did not mean financial aid: Sophia used to come early in the morning, kindle the fire, sweep the room, and dust off the girls' desks; and, in this way, earned her education. Being industrious, she could rightfully be praised by all but the "very proud and foolish girls" of the class (one of whom narrates the story) for her brave and noble spirit.[21]

Sophia was late in finishing her work one morning, and as the girls arrived, Julia, Kate, and the narrator began to tease her with the feather-duster. "Sophia bore all this very patiently as long as she could," but when the girls decided to plunder the teacher's desk, Sophia voiced her disapproval. "Who are you, I wonder, to dare say *we* shan't do what we like?" cried one of the girls. A tussle ensued, and Julia knocked an inkstand off a desk, spilling ink onto the carpet. Shock and terror followed. Only Sophia had the presence of mind and the willingness to begin cleaning up the ink, which she was still doing when Miss Adams, the teacher, came into the room. Miss Adams sharply reproved Sophia and warned her that she might not be allowed to continue in her employment if she could not be more careful.

> Sophia burst into tears at the rebuke of her kind teacher. It seemed too much to be borne; and she was tempted to tell the whole story, and let the blame fall where it belonged. But she called to mind the text: *'Be not overcome of evil; but overcome evil with good.'*
>
> This calmed her feeling, and she meekly said: 'Miss Adams, it was an accident. I am very sorry, and will try never to let it happen again;' and then went home for some water and a clean cloth, to wash out the ugly stains.[22]

The subtext is worth noting. The teacher did not ask what had happened when she entered the room. Rather, she assumed that Sophia was the guilty party. After all, Sophia was cleaning up the spill and, being poor, one could more easily believe that she was capable of such clumsiness. The teacher's presumption of guilt was morally little different from the girls' outrage over Sophia's presumptuousness. Still, Sophia chose to act in a Christ-like fashion: she remembered scripture, accepted the censure, and proceeded to wash away the stains of others. One doubts that her word would have been believed had she accused the other girls anyway.

Sophia's noble conduct put the other girls to shame, and they accordingly made a full confession. Then follows the moral of the story:

> We should never despise the condition of those who are less favored than ourselves. The poor have to endure many hardships, and we should try, at all times, to do them all the good we can.

The story is followed by a set of questions, the last question asking, "How ought we treat the poor?" One can only conclude that the honest poor deserved respect as they struggled to work their way out of poverty.[23]

Stories set outside the home and the classroom more often featured boys. "The Gold Sovereign," also related in *Sanders' Union Reader, Number Three*, tells of a boy named William who was bound by his poor parents to work on the farm of an honest but stern church deacon. Life with the deacon was earnest, as William later recalled:

> I did not have a very easy time; for deacon Webb believed in keeping boys at *work*, and did not mean to spoil them by allowing them much time to play. The deacon was not to allow me any thing for my services, except my food, clothing, and three months' schooling in winter; and, therefore, I did not see any money, except a few pennies which the deacon would sometimes give me.[24]

One evening, as he returned from an errand to the village store, William found a small paper package in which was wrapped a gold coin of great value. The boy was first awestruck and then delighted at his good fortune. His only worry was that someone would claim the money; or worse, that Mr. Webb would somehow be able to figure out that William had come into its possession. William's nerves began to fray. Whenever the deacon called, he jumped for fear that his secret had been discovered. The appearance of the constable convinced him that he was about to be arrested. Even a reprimand for tardiness proved to be a pleasure because it meant he was not being asked to give over the coin. Even so, William could not escape the feeling that his wealth was ill-gotten, and it made him miserable.

The truth finally came out. A poor neighbor named Mr. Baldwin, who supported his family by heavy labor, came to Mr. Webb's house for a day of work. At breakfast, Mr. Baldwin sorrowfully told of his misfortune in losing a gold coin he had carefully wrapped in paper after receiving it from the constable for another job. It was the first sovereign he had ever had, and he could ill "afford to lose [his] honest earnings." Hesitantly at first, then with more courage, William pulled the coin out of his pocket and asked Mr. Baldwin if it was his.

> I burst into tears, and confessed every thing. I expected the deacon would severely chastise me. But he patted my head, and said, in a kind tone of voice: 'Don't cry, William. You are an honest boy, if you did come near falling into temptation. Always be honest, my son, and, if you do not become rich, you will be happy with a clear conscience.'

William need not have worried. Growing in the deacon's favor, he received an inheritance of $500 when Mr. Webb died. With the money, he was able to buy quite a bit of productive farmland. That fact, William says, is not part of his story. "All I have to add is, I never regretted clearing my conscience of poor Job Baldwin's sovereign."[25] Only at the end are we offered an oblique biblical reference: like poor Job of the Old Testament, Mr. Baldwin must have been a virtuous man. He certainly was better served by his young friend than his biblical namesake was by his. William deserved the good treatment he received from Mr. Webb for his honesty. Still, one can imagine a young reader observing that he was also rather fortunate to have worked for someone with so considerable a fortune.

Students in the common schools of the young republic were well served by their textbooks. Frequently simplistic in their teachings and simply, if at all, illustrated, the textbooks were also able to bring a world of knowledge and experience into the lives of students whose homes may have contained only a Bible and an almanac. Many of the more advanced readers consisted of excerpts from the popular literature of the day. Even when stories were transparent in their teachings, they rarely patronized students. Instead, the very eagerness of the texts attests to a shared belief that the children who read them would one day become the citizens upon whom the nation would depend. Even if they advocated attitudes not in accord with all elements of a society in flux, the textbooks of the common school movement embodied a certainty that few at the time who aspired to middle-class security were willing to dispute: Education offered the best hope for the preparation of a citizenry ready to meet the opportunities of a challenging yet promising future.

We should do so well. In order for our generation's textbooks—indeed, for our schools—to help prepare students to live as adults we are required to envision something of the future they will inhabit. If we can say anything about it with confidence, we can assume it will be different from the past in at least one significant way: the unanimity of spirit expressed in the textbooks of the common school will be no more. It never existed, only in an earlier day of greater formalized disempowerment it was easier to pretend it did. Today it does not, and, in the flight of too many in our society to escape the differences of those not like them, we undervalue one of public education's great glories: its promise to bring a diverse people together in order that we might learn the things that unite us. From this perspective, the stories that yield our distinctive identities—even (or maybe especially) those which remind us of our failings—serve the greater purpose of drawing us closer to one another as we seek to realize our shared dreams of life, liberty, and the pursuit of happiness.

Notes

[1] The quotation is from the closing lines of Lincoln's First Inaugural Address. Lincoln 224.

[2] For McGuffey Readers sales figures, see Joel Spring, *The American School, 1642–1990: Varieties of Historical Interpretation of the Foundations and Development of American Education*, 2nd ed. (New York: Longman, 1990) 144.

[3] Bureau of the Census, *Manufactures of the United States in 1860* (Washington, D. C.: Department of the Interior, 1865) cxxxvii.

[4] For a parallel view, see Carl F. Kaestle's argument that the ideology of the common schools centered on "republicanism, Protestantism, and capitalism" in his *Pillars of the Republic: Common Schools and American Society, 1780–1860* (New York: Hill and Wang, 1983) 76.

[5] Quoted in Polly Welts Kaufman, *Women Teachers on the Frontier* (New Haven: Yale University Press, 1984) 188.

[6] Quoted in Kaufman 172.

[7] Quoted in Nancy Hoffman, *Woman's 'True' Profession: Voices from the History of Teaching* (New York: The Feminist Press, 1981) 33.

[8] Quoted in Spring 90.

[9] Daniel Adams, *Adams' Geography: Or, A Description of the World. In Three Parts*, 14th ed. (Boston: Lincoln & Edmands, 1832) 108.

[10] Adams 141.

[11] Congregationalist minister Jedidiah Morse (1761–1826) wrote the first and most influential geography textbook for the United States. His best known work was *The American Geography* (1789; subsequently titled *The American Universal Geography*). His eldest son was the inventor Samuel F. B. Morse. The editorial is

taken from a reprint appearing in the *Asheville News* (Asheville, North Carolina), 26 January 1860.

[12] Marcius Willson, *History of the United States* (New York: Ivison & Phinney, 1857 [1853]). One of many reminders that the official ideology of the schools was always (then, as now) supplemented by a host of often unrecognized aspirations appears in this bit of doggerel penciled on one of this copy's flyleaves:

> May you always be happy
> Live at your ease
> Get a kind husband
> And do as you please.

[13] Willson 372–4.

[14] Lyman Cobb, *Cobb's Sequel to the Juvenile Readers; Comprising a Selection of Lessons in Prose and Poetry from Highly Esteemed American and English Writers* (Baltimore: Cushing & Brother, 1847 [1832]).

[15] Cobb 123.

[16] Revelation 3:14–6 KJV.

[17] Cobb 124–6.

[18] Cobb 126.

[19] Cobb 126.

[20] Charles W. Sanders, *Sanders' Union Reader, Number Three* (New York: Ivison, Phinney, Blakeman & Co., 1862).

[21] Sanders 164.

[22] Sanders 164–6.

[23] Sanders 166–7.

[24] Sanders 210.

[25] Sanders 214–7.

Afterword

To teach is to be constantly aware of the gap between one's ideals and the reality in which we must live. The tension between ideal and reality has been apparent, at least for me, at many places in this book—finding one's voice through the institution of the public school, for example, or the approaches to teaching history that include the use of historical artifacts and critical reading of historical sources. I am the first to admit that there are times when the exigencies of simply getting through a day, crammed with too many students and bearing too many hurts to heal, offer ample justification for relying on rote learning and prepackaged lesson plans.

That said, the enormous challenge of bringing one's dreams closer to realization is too often dismissed as an impossible undertaking, as if even an honest but incomplete attempt will bring nothing but disappointment and frustration and no hope of fresh insight. "All or nothing" fits well within the American notion of success, by which we are urged to live frenetically until we come to an end at which we somehow exit quickly and quietly. The world of complete and perfect realization is not ours, however, and to allow this reality to disillusion us is to ignore the potentialities surrounding us.

There exist today precious few places other than public schools where a civil society is nurtured. If we continue to loosen our commitment to schools, either by neglecting them or balkanizing them so that only some are adequately supported, we will give lie to the democratic ideals which are so easy to dismiss but on which this nation has sustained itself. Nothing new is expressed in saying this; yet the perennial question of what an individual can do remains. We may well be living in days like the latter ones of the Roman Empire, where outward forms remained while the framework crumbled from within. In such a time, perhaps it is too much to ask that our concerns include those of our brothers and sisters, who are legion. Nevertheless, if we fail to, the prospect grows dimmer still, as none of us remains secure where all of us are not. I did not begin my teaching career thinking this way, but I believe that coming to these thoughts has given meaning to what I have done. Whenever I run into a student I once taught, I expect that the history learned in class has been largely forgotten, but something else, more elusive and more valuable, often remains. If that individual is a little more secure in his or her identity, is sometimes willing to ask hard questions, and is somewhat more understanding of stories different from his or her own, then the work was worthwhile. Even if it does not save the world, this teaching is about more than simply making one's garden grow, for I am reminded that as we ignore our ties to each other we lose our humanity.

Bibliography

Adams, Daniel. *Adams' Geography: Or, A Description of the World. In Three Parts*. 14th ed. Boston: Lincoln & Edmands, 1832.

Alderfer, E. G. *The Ephrata Commune: An Early American Counter-culture*. Pittsburgh: University of Pittsburgh Press, 1985.

Alsberg, Henry G., ed. *The American Guide: A Source Book and Complete Travel Guide for the United States*. New York: Hastings House, 1949.

Apple, Michael W. *Education and Power*. New York: Routledge and Kegan Paul, 1983.

Appleby, Joyce, Lynn Hunt, and Margaret Jacob. *Telling the Truth about History*. New York: W. W. Norton & Company, 1994.

Aronowitz, Stanley, and Henry A. Giroux. "Schooling, Culture, and Literacy in the Age of Broken Dreams: A Review of Bloom and Hirsch." *Harvard Educational Review* 58 (April 1988): 172–94.

Asheville News (Asheville, North Carolina), 26 January 1860, North Carolina State Archives.

Ayers, Edward L. *The Promise of the New South: Life After Reconstruction*. New York: Oxford University Press, 1992.

Ball, Edward. *Slaves in the Family*. New York: Farrar Straus & Giroux, 1998.

Barger, M. Susan, and William B. White. *The Daguerreotype: Nineteenth-Century Technology and Modern Science*. Washington, D. C.: Smithsonian Institution Press, 1991.

Baumgarten, Linda. *Eighteenth-Century Clothing at Williamsburg*. Williamsburg, Va.: Colonial Williamsburg Foundation, 1986.

Benjamin, Walter. "Theses on the Philosophy of History." *Illuminations*. Ed. Hannah Arendt. New York: Schocken Books, 1969.

Berkin, Carol, Alan Brinkley, Clayborne Carson, Robert W. Cherny, Robert A. Divine, Eric Foner, Jeffrey B. Morris, The Reverend Arthur Wheeler, C.S.C., and Leonard Wood. *American Voices: A History of the United States*. Glenview, Illinois: Scott, Foresman and Company, 1992.

Berman, Marshall. *All That Is Solid Melts Into Air: The Experience of Modernity*. New York: Simon and Schuster, 1982.

Betts, Edwin Morris, ed. *Thomas Jefferson's Farm Book*. Charlottesville: University Press of Virginia, 1987.

Bolton, Charles C. *Poor Whites of the Antebellum South: Tenants and Laborers in Central North Carolina and Northeast Mississippi*. Durham, N. C.: Duke University Press, 1994.

Bolton, Charles C., and Scott P. Culclasure, eds. *The Confessions of Edward Isham: A Poor White Life of the Old South*. Athens, Georgia: University of Georgia Press, 1998.

Bridenbaugh, Carl. "Violence and Virtue in Virginia, 1766; or, The Importance of the Trivial." *Early Americans*. Ed. Carl Bridenbaugh. New York: Oxford University Press, 1981.

Britzman, Deborah P. *Practice Makes Perfect: A Critical Study of Learning*. Albany: State University of New York Press, 1991.

Burton, Orville Vernon. *In My Father's House Are Many Mansions: Family and Community in Edgefield, South Carolina*. Chapel Hill: University of North Carolina Press, 1985.

Burton, Robert. *The Anatomy of Melancholy*. New York: Farrar & Rinehart, 1927.

Bynum, Victoria E. *Unruly Women: The Politics of Social and Sexual Control in the Old South*. Chapel Hill: University of North Carolina Press, 1992.

Calhoon, Robert M. *Evangelicals and Conservatives in the Early South, 1740–1861*. Columbia: University of South Carolina Press, 1988.

Civil War, The,: Original Soundtrack Recording. Elektra Nonesuch 9–79256–2.

Cobb, Lyman. *Cobb's Sequel to the Juvenile Readers; Comprising a Selection of Lessons in Prose and Poetry from Highly Esteemed American and English Writers*. Baltimore: Cushing & Brother, 1847 [1832].

Collections of the Genealogical Society of Pennsylvania: Abstracts of Lancaster County, Pennsylvania, Wills, 1721–1820.

Collingwood, R. G. *The Idea of History*. Oxford: University Press, 1946.

Committee for the Compilation of Materials on Damage Caused by the Atomic Bombs, The, ed. *Hiroshima and Nagasaki: The Physical, Medical, and Social Effects of the Atomic Bombings*. New York: Basic Books, Inc., Publishers, 1981.

Confederate Military Service Records. National Archives, Washington, D. C.

Cook, Haruko Taya and Theodore F. Cook. *Japan at War: An Oral History*. New York: The New Press, 1992.

Cook, Raymond Allen. *Fire from the Flint: The Amazing Careers of Thomas Dixon*. Winston-Salem, North Carolina: John F. Blair, Publisher, 1968.

Culclasure, Scott P. "'I Have Killed a Damned Dog': Murder by a Poor White in the Antebellum South." *North Carolina Historical Review* LXX (January 1993): 14–39.

———. "Edward Isham and Criminal Justice for the Poor White in Antebellum North Carolina." *Journal of Southern Legal History* III (1994): 71–96.

Current, Richard Nelson. *Arguing with Historians: Essays on the Historical and the Unhistorical*. Middletown, Connecticut: Wesleyan University Press, 1987.

———. *Those Terrible Carpetbaggers: A Reinterpretation*. New York: Oxford University Press, 1988.

Darnton, Robert. *The Great Cat Massacre*. New York: Random House, 1985.

———. *The Forbidden Best-Sellers of Pre-Revolutionary France*. New York: W. W. Norton, 1995.

———. "Cherchez la Femme." Rev. of *Monsieur d'Eon Is a Woman: A Tale of Political Intrigue and Sexual Masquerade*, by Gary Kates. *The New York Review of Books* 10 August 1995: 22.

De Tocqueville, Alexis. *Democracy in America*. Trans. George Lawrence. Ed. J. P. Mayer. New York: Anchor Books, 1969.

Deetz, James. *Flowerdew Hundred: The Archaeology of a Virginia Plantation, 1619–1864*. Charlottesville: University of Virginia Press, 1993.

Demos, John. *The Unredeemed Captive: A Family Story from Early America*. New York: Alfred A. Knopf, 1994.

Dewey, John. *Democracy and Education: An Introduction to the Philosophy of Education*. New York: The Macmillan Company, 1916.

Dixon, Thomas, Jr. *The Leopard's Spots: A Romance of the White Man's Burden—1865–1900*. New York: Doubleday, Page & Company, 1902.

———. *The One Woman: A Story of Modern Utopia*. New York: Doubleday, Page & Company, 1903.

———. *The Clansman: An Historical Romance of the Ku Klux Klan*. New York: Doubleday, Page & Company, 1905.

———. *The Black Hood*. New York: D. Appleton and Company, 1924.

———. *The Flaming Sword*. Atlanta, Georgia: Monarch Publishing Company, 1939.

Donald, David Herbert. *Lincoln*. New York: Simon and Schuster, 1995.

Douglass, Frederick. *Autobiographies*. New York: Library of America, 1994.

Du Bois, W. E. B. *Writings*. New York: Library of America, 1986.

Durnbaugh, Donald F. *The Believers' Church: The History and Character of Radical Protestantism*. New York: Macmillan, 1968.

Eco, Umberto. *The Island of the Day Before*. New York: Harcourt Brace & Company, 1995.

Egan, Timothy. "Many Seek Security in Private Communities." *The New York Times* 3 September 1995: A1.

"1851 Orangeburg District Tax List." *The South Carolina Magazine of Ancestral Research* VII (1979): 18-21.

Eliot, T. S. *Four Quartets*. New York: Harcourt Brace & Company, 1943.

Faulkner, William. *Absalom, Absalom!* in *Novels, 1936–1940*. New York: Library of America, 1990.

Fischer, David Hackett. *Paul Revere's Ride*. New York: Oxford University Press, 1994.

Fleischhauer, Carl, and Beverly W. Brannan, ed. *Documenting America, 1935–1943*. Berkeley: University of California Press, 1988.

Foner, Eric. *Reconstruction: America's Unfinished Revolution, 1863–1877*. New York: Harper & Row, 1988.

Foucault, Michael. *Power/Knowledge: Selected Interviews and Other Writings, 1972–1977*. New York: Pantheon Books, 1980.

———. "What Is Enlightenment?" *The Foucault Reader*. Ed. Paul Rabinow. New York: Pantheon, 1984.

Frazier, Charles. *Cold Mountain*. New York: Atlantic Monthly Press, 1997.

Freire, Paulo. *Pedagogy of the Oppressed*. New York: Continuum Publishing Company, 1970.

Giroux, Henry A. "Critical Pedagogy, Cultural Politics, and the Discourse of Experience." *Curriculum: An Introduction to the Field*. Ed. James R. Gress amd David E. Purpel. Berkeley, California: McCutchan Publishing Corporation, 1988.

———. *Teachers As Intellectuals: Toward a Critical Pedagogy of Learning*. South Hadley, Massachusetts: Bergin and Garvey, 1990.

Glasgow, Ellen. *In This Our Life*. New York: Harcourt Brace and Company, 1941.

———. *A Certain Measure: An Interpretation of Prose Fiction*. New York: Harcourt Brace and Company, 1943.

Governors Letter Books, North Carolina State Archives.

Governors Papers, North Carolina State Archives.

Hackett, Alice Payne. *Fifty Years of Best Sellers, 1895–1945*. New York: R. R. Bowker Co., 1945.

Hahn, Steven. *The Roots of Southern Populism: Yeomen Farmers and the Transformation of the Georgia Upcountry, 1850–1890*. New York: Oxford University Press, 1983.

Hahn, Steven, and Jonathan Prude, eds. *The Countryside in the Age of Capitalist Transformation: Essays in the Social History of Rural America*. Chapel Hill: University of North Carolina Press, 1985.

Hakim, Joy. *A History of US*. 2d ed. 10 vols. New York: Oxford University Press, 1999.

Hall, Jacquelyn Dowd, James Leloudis, Robert Korstad, Mary Murphy, Lu Ann Jones, and Christopher B. Daly. *Like a Family: The Making of a Southern Cotton Mill World*. Chapel Hill: University of North Carolina Press, 1987.

Harvey, David. *The Condition of Postmodernity: An Enquiry into the Origins of Cultural Change*. New York: Basil Blackwell Ltd., 1989.

Herman, Michele. "The Electronic Toaster." *American Heritage* 41 (December 1990): 36–7.

Heschel, Abraham Joshua. *The Sabbath: Its Meaning for Modern Man*. New York: Farrar, Straus and Giroux, 1951.

Hoffman, Nancy. *Woman's 'True' Profession: Voices from the History of Teaching*. New York: The Feminist Press, 1981.

hooks, bell. "Postmodern Blackness." *The Truth About the Truth: De-Confusing and Re-Constructing the Postmodern World*. Ed. Walter Truett Anderson. New York: G. P. Putnam's Sons, 1995.

Humphreys, Hugh C. "'Agitate! Agitate! Agitate!': The Great Fugitive Slave Law Convention and Its Rare Daguerreotype." *Madison County Heritage* 19 (Oneida, New York: Madison County Historical Society, 1994).

Kaestle, Carl F. *Pillars of the Republic: Common Schools and American Society, 1780–1860*. New York: Hill and Wang, 1983.

Kaufman, Polly Welts. *Women Teachers on the Frontier*. New Haven: Yale University Press, 1984.

Knoblock, Steve, ed. "Cartes de Visites: A Social Revolution." <http://www.webcom/cityg/earlyphoto/articles/Cartes_de_Visite_A_Social_Revolution.html>. 16 March 1998.

Lange, Dorothea. "The Assignment I'll Never Forget." *Popular Photography* 46, no. 2 (February 1960): 42–3, 126.

Lasch, Christopher. *The True and Only Heaven: Progress and Its Critics*. New York: W. W. Norton & Company, 1991.

Lerner. Gerda. *Why History Matters: Life and Thought*. New York: Oxford University Press, 1997.

Lerner, Michael. *Jewish Renewal: A Path to Healing and Transformation*. New York: G. P. Putnam's Sons, 1994.

Library of Congress. "American Memory." 27 November 1997. <http://lcweb2.loc.gov/ammem.html>. 16 February 1998.

Lincoln, Abraham. *Speeches and Writings, 1859–1865*. New York: Library of America, 1989.

Litwack, Leon F. *Trouble in Mind: Black Southerners in the Age of Jim Crow*. New York: Alfred A. Knopf, 1998.

McClendon, Carlee T., comp. *Edgefield Marriage Records, Edgefield, South Carolina: From the Late Eighteenth Century up through 1870*. Columbia, South Carolina: R. L. Bryan, 1970.

———. *Edgefield Death Notices and Cemetery Records*. Columbia, South Carolina: Hive Press, 1977.

McLaurin, Melton A. *Separate Pasts: Growing Up White in the Segregated South*. Athens, Georgia: University of Georgia Press, 1987.

———. *Celia, A Slave*. (Athens, Georgia: University of Georgia Press, 1991.

Metz, Johann-Baptist. "The Future in the Memory of Suffering." *Faith and the Future: Essays on Theology, Solidarity, and Modernity*. Ed. Johann-Baptist Metz and Jürgen Moltmann. Maryknoll, New York: Orbis Books, 1995.

Morgan, Edmund S. *American Slavery, American Freedom: The Ordeal of Colonial Virginia.* New York: W. W. Norton & Company, 1975.

National Archives Trust Fund Board. *The American Image: Photographs from the National Archives, 1860–1960.* Intro. Alan Trachtenberg. New York: Pantheon Books, 1979.

Newhall, Beaumont. *The Daguerreotype in America.* New York: Dover Publication, Inc., 1976.

North Carolina Standard (Raleigh), 20 April 1853, North Carolina State Archives.

Olsen, Otto H. *Carpetbagger's Crusade: The Life of Albion Winegar Tourgée.* Baltimore: Johns Hopkins Press, 1965.

Pagano, Jo Anne. *Exiles and Communities: Teaching in the Patriarchal Wilderness.* Albany: State University of New York Press, 1990.

Perrot, Michelle, ed. *A History of Private Life,* vol. IV, *From the Fires of Revolution to the Great War.* Cambridge, Massachusetts: The Belknap Press of Harvard University Press, 1990.

Preston, Douglas. "All the King's Sons." *The New Yorker* 22 January 1996: 44–59.

Redford, Dorothy Spruill. *Somerset Homecoming: Recovering a Lost Heritage.* New York: Anchor Books Doubleday, 1988.

Rosengarten, Theodore. *All God's Dangers: The Life of Nate Shaw.* New York: Alfred A. Knopf, 1974.

Russell, Francis. *The Shadow of Blooming Grove: Warren G. Harding in His Times.* New York: McGraw-Hill Book Company, 1968.

Sanders, Charles W. *Sanders' Union Reader, Number Three.* New York: Ivison, Phinney, Blakeman & Co., 1862.

Schama, Simon. *Landscape and Memory.* New York: Alfred A. Knopf, 1995.

David Schenck Books, Southern Historical Collection, University of North Carolina Library, Chapel Hill.

David Schenck Papers, North Carolina State Archives.

Schenck, David. *North Carolina, 1780–'81; Being a History of the Invasion of the Carolinas by the British*. Raleigh, N. C.: Edwards & Broughton, 1889.

———. *A Memorial Volume of the Guilford Battle Ground Company*. Greensboro, N. C.: Charles L. Van Noppen, 1893.

Shapiro, Svi. *Between Capitalism and Democracy: Educational Policy and the Crisis of the Welfare State*. South Hadley, Massachusetts: Bergin and Garvey, 1990.

Smithsonian Books. *Images of America: A Panorama of History in Photographs*. Washington, D. C.: Smithsonian Books, 1989.

Solomon, Maynard. *Beethoven*. New York: Schirmer Books, 1977.

Spring, Joel. *The American School, 1642–1990: Varieties of Historical Interpretation of the Foundations and Development of American Education*. 2nd ed. New York: Longman, 1990.

Stone, Alfred E. *Autobiographical Occasions and Original Acts: Versions of American Identity from Henry Adams to Nate Shaw*. Philadelphia: University of Pennsylvania Press, 1982.

Strassler, Sobert B., ed. *The Landmark Thucydides: A Comprehensive Guide to the Pelopponesian War*. New York: The Free Press, 1996.

Thomas, Benjamin P. *Lincoln: A Biography*. New York: Alfred A. Knopf, 1952.

Thompson, E. P. *Customs in Common: Studies in Traditional Popular Culture*. New York: The New Press, 1991.

Thorp, Willard. *A Southern Reader*. New York: Alfred A. Knopf, 1955.

Toastmaster Incorporated. <http://www.toastmaster.com>. 27 December 1997.

Albion W. Tourgée Papers. Chautauqua County Historical Society, Westfield, New York. Microfilm, University of North Carolina at Greensboro.

Tourgée, Albion W. *A Fool's Errand, By One of the Fools*. New York: Fords, Howard, and Hulbert, 1879.

———. *A Fool's Errand and the Invisible Empire*. New York: Fords, Howard, and Hulbert, 1880.

———. *Bricks Without Straw: A Novel*. New York: Fords, Howard, and Hulbert, 1880.

———. *An Appeal to Caesar*. New York: Fords, Howard, and Hulbert, 1884.

Trachtenberg, Alan. *Reading American Photographs: Images as History, Mathew Brady to Walker Evans*. New York: Hill and Wang, 1989.

Tullos, Allen. *Habits of Industry: White Culture and the Transformation of the Carolina Piedmont*. Chapel Hill: University of North Carolina Press, 1989.

U. S. Bureau of the Census. *Manufactures of the United States in 1860*. Washington, D. C.: Department of the Interior, 1865.

U. S. Bureau of the Census, Federal Manuscript Censuses, 1850, 1860, 1870, 1880, Catawba, Iredell, Wake counties, North Carolina. Microfilm.

U. S. Bureau of the Census, Federal Manuscript Censuses, 1830, 1840, 1860, 1870, 1880, 1910, Edgefield, Orangeburg counties, South Carolina. Microfilm.

U. S. Bureau of the Census, Federal Manuscript Censuses, 1820, Albemarle County, Virginia. Microfilm.

"Voice of Hibakusha." 22 April 1994. <http://129.171.129.67/mf/hibakusha/index.html>. 15 April 1998.

Ward, Geoffrey C., with Ric Burns and Ken Burns. *The Civil War: An Illustrated History*. New York: Alfred A. Knopf, 1990.

Welch, Sharon D. *Communities of Resistance and Solidarity: A Feminist Theology of Liberation*. Maryknoll, New York: Orbis Books, 1985.

White, George Abbott. "The Hem of My Garment: An Interview with Theodore Rosengarten about the Makings of 'Nate Shaw,'" *The Massachusetts Review* XXI (Winter 1980): 787-8.

Willson, Marcius. *History of the United States*. New York: Ivison & Phinney, 1857 [1853].

Wyatt-Brown, Bertram. *Southern Honor: Ethics and Behavior in the Old South*. New York: Oxford University Press, 1982.

Zinn, Howard. *A People's History of the United States, 1492–Present*, rev. ed. New York: HarperPerennial, 1995.

COUNTERPOINTS

Studies in the Postmodern Theory of Education

General Editors
Joe L. Kincheloe & Shirley R. Steinberg

Counterpoints publishes the most compelling and imaginative books being written in education today. Grounded on the theoretical advances in criticalism, feminism, and postmodernism in the last two decades of the twentieth century, Counterpoints engages the meaning of these innovations in various forms of educational expression. Committed to the proposition that theoretical literature should be accessible to a variety of audiences, the series insists that its authors avoid esoteric and jargonistic languages that transform educational scholarship into an elite discourse for the initiated. Scholarly work matters only to the degree it affects consciousness and practice at multiple sites. Counterpoints' editorial policy is based on these principles and the ability of scholars to break new ground, to open new conversations, to go where educators have never gone before.

For additional information about this series or for the submission of manuscripts, please contact:

Joe L. Kincheloe & Shirley R. Steinberg
637 West Foster Avenue
State College, PA 16801

To order other books in this series, please contact our Customer Service Department at:

(800) 770-LANG (within the U.S.)
(212) 647-7706 (outside the U.S.)
(212) 647-7707 FAX

or browse online by series at:

www.peterlang.com

